THE RESIDENTS AND
OTHER UNIQUE SENIORS

THE RESIDENTS AND OTHER UNIQUE SENIORS

EUNIE GUYRE

authorHOUSE®

AuthorHouse™ LLC
1663 Liberty Drive
Bloomington, IN 47403
www.authorhouse.com
Phone: 1-800-839-8640

Published by AuthorHouse   01/06/2014

ISBN: 978-1-4918-4846-3 (sc)
ISBN: 978-1-4918-4847-0 (e)

Library of Congress Control Number: 2014900119

Table of Contents

Section One

The Residents

Section Two

Other Unique Seniors

Section Three
Fleeting Thoughts and Random Senior Moments

Dedication

This book is dedicated to the people who touched my heart, made me smile, made me laugh, sometimes made me cry, and forever enriched my life.

Disclaimer

If some of these folks resemble your loved ones in any way,
please know they are, and were, loved very much.

SECTION ONE
The Residents

Maureen

*M*aureen, an Irish beauty despite her advanced age, has just entered her new room at the nursing facility. She has red hair, bright blue eyes and a few freckles sprinkled across her nose amid the age spots on her face. The woman is friendly and at ease, as she checks out her new surroundings. I introduce myself to the nervous woman who accompanies her. She is Maureen's daughter and I try to ease the worry from her face.

"I am one of the nurses' aides here who will get to see your mother just about every day," I tell her. "We will become friends very quickly. I can feel it already."

I turn to my new resident and ask if she likes to sing and dance.

"Oh, sure I do! I worked at a bar in town for years. Everybody knows me, if you know what I mean!" As we become engaged in conversation, her daughter interrupts briefly to say, "Mom, I have to run some errands now. I'll be back to see you later. Okay?" "Okay!" her mom answers cheerfully.

Maureen turns back to me and fills me in on her "job" at the bar, hardly noticing her daughter's exit. "I guess I was kind of known as a floozy back then. I really *was*, too!" She laughs, bending her head back, her hair brushing her shoulders.

This woman has clearly been sent to me by the fun god; I can feel it!

As we unpack her bag, she holds up a scarf and twirls it around her shoulders, then holds a bright paisley blouse against her as she admires herself in the mirror.

Maureen has a small, pretty box filled with costume jewelry that she places on her bedside table. She sits in her recliner, sorting out her gems. Earrings and pins of every color are filling up her table as I leave this busy, happy woman.

I have a few minutes before my shift ends to check out the chart displaying Maureen's history. To my surprise, she has not been a floozy at all; in fact has never worked in a bar. She is a much-loved community volunteer and devoted mother to eight children.

I leave for home a little disappointed by this revelation and plan to play along with Maureen's version of her life when I see her tomorrow.

Roberta

$\mathcal{R}$oberta has been living here at the nursing home for about a week. She is a lovely woman who enjoys visits from her daughter every afternoon. She gets around pretty well, but is on oxygen constantly and rings her buzzer when she needs to go to the bathroom because she fears tripping on the tubing.

Because Roberta reminds me of a much-loved neighbor who has passed away, I stop by her room frequently to chat for a few minutes. She is bright and alert and I enjoy her company very much.

I am delighted one morning when she is one of the residents assigned for me to take care of and help with her washing up and getting dressed.

Because it is important for residents to do as much for themselves as they can, I hand Roberta a soapy washcloth to wash her upper body as I wash her back. She tells me, "I'll wash *Possible.*" I don't know what she means, but don't ask. I wonder if she is confused due to lack of oxygen or something and I have not realized this before.

As she dries herself, I wash her legs and feet and begin to put panties, slacks, socks and shoes on her. Again she says, "I'll wash *Possible.*"

When she stands up, she washes her private parts and when she is finished dressing, we walk back to her recliner chair. *She* doesn't seem confused, but *I* am. I wish her a good morning and go on my way.

The nurse laughs when I tell her I am dismayed to find that Roberta isn't as "with it" as I had thought.

Nurse Kathy, a long-time caregiver to the elderly, explains, "Some residents call their privates *Possible* because aides tell them 'wash yourself as far down as possible and I'll do the rest'."

Who knew?

I am relieved to know what is possible.

Tessa

"*Hello.* Come join me on the piazza", Tessa invites.

Having just finished my lunch, I tell her I'll be back as soon as I bring my empty coffee cup into the kitchen. She nods her head and waits patiently for me with her hands loosely folded on her lap.

I sit beside this dear little lady in her yellow flowered housecoat, her long, fly-away white hair hanging over her shoulders and chest. She has a wistful smile on her face today

She tells me, "I love being here at Lake Wentworth with my father. See the trees and hear the birds?"

"It *is* lovely here", I agree. I take it all in for a while as we both sit quietly.

I almost lift the teacup to my lips from the small wicker table in front of us.

But there *is* no teacup; there is no wicker table.

I come back in the moment and realize, she is in her wheelchair, and I am kneeling on the floor getting ready to take her blood pressure.

Tessa pulls me in so completely, I momentarily forget she is blind and we are in the lobby of a nursing home.

Alma

Alma tells me about her honeymoon with her sexy, handsome new husband; how they never tired of making love, "every single night up until he died."

I ask, "How long were you married, Alma?"

"Sixty years."

"Yes, its true", she assures me as I help her bathe, dress, and comb her hair. The twinkle in 88-year old Alma's eyes is still bright.

"*God, I wish I had Superman in my life*," I'm thinking to myself, hoping my thoughts are not showing on my face.

"That's why we have nine children," she tells me proudly.

She is especially proud of her son Robert, "a very good priest. He's pastor of a big church near here and all the people love him."

"I'd like to meet him. Does he ever get a chance to visit you during the day?" I ask.

"Oh, yes. I'll introduce you to him the next time he comes."

Alma seems unsure where her other children live.

One afternoon, she motions for me to come into her room. "This is my daughter Catherine."

"Hi", I say to the woman sitting next to Alma. It's so nice to meet you."

Later, as Catherine comes down the hallway to go home, I stop her to say, "We all love your mom. She's so proud of all of you and just lights up when she mentions your brother, the priest."

Catherine shrugs and says, "I'm an only child. Mother has always been prone to story telling."

Virginia and Betty

*V*irginia is convinced her roommate Betty is her mother in law. She always rifles through Betty's closets and drawers, checking to make sure all her clothes are neat and fashionable.

Betty rarely has much to say, and mostly wears a scowl on her face.

"Stop coming over to my side", she admonishes Virginia. "These are *my* clothes. Yours are over there," she gestures.

The aides and nurses have to keep a close watch on Virginia on the days she becomes especially rambunctious. On one such day, Virginia grabs the handles of Betty's wheelchair, and, without warning, spins her around. In a burst of energy, she steers a shouting Betty, who tries with all her might to plant her feet in front of her, in an attempt to stop this madwoman from making a beeline down the hall.

"Where are you going, Virginia?" an aide asks the pretend daughter in law.

Smiling her contagious smile, she informs her they are "taking a nice walk."

Later in the day, I come upon Betty, who is almost at the end of her seat being pushed by her roommate. I summon another aide to help me scoot Betty safely back in her chair.

"Where are you going now?" I ask. Betty does not answer. She has clearly given up the fight.

Taking my hand and pulling me towards the side of the hallway, briefly abandoning her charge, Virginia confides, "I'm going to the pay phone. I'm trying to make hotel reservations for my mother in law. She's starting to drive me crazy."

Jeannette

Jeannette Green has lived in New Hampshire her entire life. She is ninety-eight years old now, so most of her friends are gone. Her few visitors here at the nursing home are mostly members of her church.

This little lady keeps to herself, although she occasionally goes to coffee hour in the activities room. She usually spends her days sitting by the window in her room where she reads her bible.

I have worked here as an aide for about five years. This is how long I have known Jeannette, but I really don't know much about her at all. She is a woman of few words. What I *do* know about her is, she loves her "Lily of the Valley" soap and talcum powder. She also uses special cream that keeps her aged face smooth and surprisingly wrinkle-free. I only know the superficial woman. She gives away nothing of her personal life, but is a very pleasant lady. I assume all her loved ones are gone.

One afternoon, as I begin to fan fold the blanket to ready the bed for Jeannette's daily nap, she tells me, "Oh, I'm not going to bed today. I'm expecting company."

"How nice, Jeannette. Enjoy," I say, giving her a hug before leaving to answer the call lights.

Passing her room later on, I smile at the sight of the two women engaged in happy conversation. Jeannette's thick white hair resembles a large pom pom, while her visitor sports a grey, low, hippy-style pony tail. The two women seem so opposite in their styles and demeanor; Jeannette dresses like a "church lady" and is a bit uptight. Her guest is laid back with a very calm manner about her.

They don't get together often, as the visitor, I later learn, lives in Connecticut. Since she seems quite elderly, too, I am surprised she has been able to drive herself the nearly three hours it takes to get here.

I wonder how they know each other. Perhaps they are school chums. My heart warms observing them enjoying this time together. I don't ever remember Jeannette being so animated while talking to someone. Hopefully, I'll have time to ask her for all the details of their friendship after her friend departs. Maybe she'll decide to share a bit of herself with me today.

When Jeannette's bell lights up, I go to her room. She tells me, "My daughter is leaving now and I am ready for my nap."

Oh, my goodness, this woman is her daughter, I'm thinking. I cannot imagine an elderly woman having her mother still on this earth. Shock has stopped me in my tracks, nearly causing me to gasp, but I catch myself.

My surprise does not escape Jeannette.

She explains, "Sue is eighty years old. I was eighteen when she was born."

Some days, my job as a nursing assistant leaves me speechless.

Ivy

She entered the front door of the nursing home with a royal demeanor. Tall and self-assured, her much-shorter daughter holding her arm, the woman introduced herself to the receptionist.

"Hello. I am Ivy Morgan and I have a two-o'clock appointment with your head person."

Betty Anne, the receptionist, led Ivy and her daughter to the lobby, where they sat waiting for the administrator.

Some of us on staff were nearby at the nurses' station gathering blood-pressure cuffs for our afternoon rounds. We took immediate notice of our new resident-to-be. She was beautiful in the way Eleanor Roosevelt was beautiful. She was also intimidating. Most newcomers to our facility were being led by their family members. Mrs. Morgan was clearly in charge of herself.

I hoped, silently, I would not be assigned to her until more was known about why she was here and if she were going to attempt to run us all ragged.

Of course I was paged a half-hour later to help our new resident to her room. Taking a deep breath, I introduced myself to Ivy who followed silently to her new room on the West wing.

She sat in the recliner that was delivered earlier from her former home as her daughter emptied a small carry-on bag while I unpacked her suitcase.

It wasn't until I heard a shy "thank you", I turned around to observe Ivy opening a box of crayons her daughter had placed next to the coloring book on the small table.

Ivy was not what she seemed when she first walked into the home. She had dementia and was very childlike now.

We would all eventually get to know both sides of our new lady. Taking care of her made me remember that old saying, "You can't judge a book by its cover."

Lina

*O*n one of my many visits to the nursing home, I stop to talk to a woman who is sitting by herself in the Activities Room.

I introduce myself to her and she tells me her name is Lina.

She is a sad, serious woman who moved to New Hampshire from Washington to be closer to her son and his wife.

Lina misses Washington, so I sit down next to her, hoping to befriend her and see her smile.

We share the ups and downs of life and part of her story unfolds in our first conversation together.

"My first husband cheated. I wanted to divorce him, but he got cancer. I stayed with him until he died. That was six years of my life wasted."

She continues. "My second husband was wonderful. He got killed in a car accident."

This is the entire story she shares this day; brief and tragic.

Anthony

According to his wife Lucille, Anthony was quite the charmer before Alzheimer's took away his former self. During quiet moments, he could have been mistaken for Anthony Quinn, the actor. When I said this to Lucille, she told me, "We met on a cruise, and when I first laid eyes on him, he reminded me of Zorba the Greek! We loved dancing together."

Now, in the late stages of the disease, all the poor man could do was babble; not one word out of his mouth was understandable. Sometimes, he even forgot how to walk until I marched slowly next to him so he could mimic what I was doing.

Several times a day, he would empty his drawers and closet and stack all his clothes on his bed. At first, I thought he was packing to go home, but when his wife came for her daily visit, Anthony did not recognize her.

Since Lucille shared with me that the two of them loved to dance, I assumed Anthony liked music. Sure enough, I discovered the only way to get him to walk down the hallway with me for his shower was to sing. "Our:" song was, "Oh we ain't got a barrel of money . . . ." And we marched to the sound of our own voices.

There was a piano in the lobby. I brought Anthony over to sit on the bench one day and, when he began to play, I could hardly contain myself. He played the most beautiful music, with no mistakes at all. His handsome face lit up with each melody. Watching him there was like witnessing a miracle.

Roger and Mary Ann

*K*ari, one of our newer nurses' aides is assigned to Roger and Mary Ann's room. My job is to check on how she has managed caring for them for the first time.

I don't envy Kari, as the misery in this room can be felt as soon as you walk in. What a pity, I think, for a husband and wife to be spending the final years of their lives sharing this small space when they obviously can't stand one another.

When they first move into the nursing home, Roger busies himself making beautiful latch-hooked rugs at a folding table on his side of the room. After suffering a stroke, he is no longer able to pursue his hobby, and mostly sits quietly watching TV now. He manages a smile when those of us on staff he likes come in to help him get ready for the day.

None of us knows the secret to making Mary Ann smile, though. She never wants to leave the room to participate in activities or sit outside by the garden. She doesn't care about TV either. Most of her day is spent looking blankly out of her window. We try engaging her in conversation, but she answers in as few words as possible.

I am surprised by the wide, happy smile that greets us as Roger looks up when I stop by with Kari. *Great job, Kari,* I will tell her when we go back out to the hallway. Obviously, she has been a big hit with this man today!

Sadly, when we walk over to Mary Ann, she is more somber than usual. "Mary Ann, are you feeling okay?" I ask. She nods a slow *yes.* I have known her for almost a year now, and resign myself to the reality there is nothing I can do to coax any happiness out of her.

We check the bathroom to make sure all is tidy. Something catches my eye; something Kari will not have known about. Roger's green denture cup is on Mary Ann's shelf and her white one is on *his*. The third-shift aide must have absent mindedly switched them the night before.

Even though Roger is a big guy, his dentures are much smaller than Mary Ann's. This certainly explains his wide smile this morning!

When we get them straightened out, Mary Ann no longer looks quite so sad.

Kari and I hold in our giggles until we get several doorways down the hallway.

Archie

Archie Matthews is a serious, quiet man who rarely mingles with the other residents.

Anxious to persuade him to smile, Joan, a kind and caring nurse, takes extra time with him on her daily rounds.

For several weekends, on her days off, she scours flea markets, used-book shops and Goodwill stores in search of an "Archie" comic book.

Finally, she finds one and happily presents it to Archie.

His response: "Why are you giving me *this*?"

Joan replies, "Don't you remember Archie comic books? You and he have the same name."

"I *hate* my name. I'd rather be *Bob* Matthews," the ungrateful man tells the well-meaning nurse.

Joan hopes her skin will grow thicker with each shift here at the nursing home.

Lillian

Lillian is "pleasantly confused." Her little-girl demeanor warms my heart. She likes to help me choose the clothes she will wear. Her helpfulness can take some time as she changes her mind a lot about which outfit is the best one.

She follows closely as I gather the towel, soap and other toiletries we will need to get her ready for the day.

I enjoy telling her stories as she is delighted by everything I say. She looks straight into my eyes with all the attention of a little child waiting to hear what happens next.

Lillian likes to help me in the afternoon when I measure the blood pressure of my other charges. She is a wonderful assistant, carrying my stethoscope.

My husband drives me to work in his truck one morning as the winter snow storm makes driving difficult for me in my compact car.

He always wears his cowboy hat to keep the blowing snow off his face.

When he steps into the lobby later that afternoon to bring me home from work, I tell Lillian, "That's my husband."

"Can I meet him?" she asks shyly.

"Of course you can," I tell her as I take her hand and lead her to the doorway.

Excitement and wonderment flashes across her face as she extends her hand to him and says, "I'm *very* glad to meet you."

Turning to me, Lillian says, "You didn't tell me your husband is a cowboy. I've never met a *real* cowboy before!"

I hug her good-bye, and when I turn to climb into the truck, I see Lillian standing at the lobby window, waving enthusiastically to the cowboy.

Paula

$\mathcal{B}$ecause I have been volunteering at a local nursing home for a little over a year, most of the folks who live there know me pretty well. For about an hour, one Sunday a month, we have coffee together and share memories. My visit is on the activities calendar as "Coffee with Eunie."

Since most of them are unable to venture too far from the facility, I enjoy informing the residents about all the changes that are taking place here in town; the new stores, the rail trail and letting them know what is available at all the craft fairs in the area.

Paula always participates in whatever we are discussing. Since she is one of the "leaders of the pack" of women who greet visitors to the home, she is in charge of reading from the daily calendar so everyone will know what is on tap for the day.

Upon my early arrival last month, I listened to Paula's announcement over the public address system.

"Good morning. Today is Sunday, October fourteenth. At nine-fifteen, there will be room visits with Jean." Then, with great excitement, she announces, "At ten o'clock, we will meet in activities for coffee with urine!"

Grandma

A sweet little ninety-five year old woman we call "Grandma", lives at the nursing home where I work.

She is fragile, but very alert mentally. The staff enjoys her wonderful sense of humor as well as her sound advice. When any of us is having a bad day, it always gets better after spending time with Grandma.

Early one afternoon, while walking past her room with another aide, we hear: "Ohh, ohh, ohh . . ."

Fearing the worst, we rush in to find Grandma, unhurt, sitting in her chair enthusiastically singing the popular song written in 1911: "Ohh, ohh, ohh, ohh, you great big beautiful doll!"

Edie and Cathleen

The nurses at a nursing home heard residents, Edie and Cathleen arguing. They usually commented about people walking past, but today were criticizing each other. Their loud accusations grew stronger.

"Your husband never could keep a decent job, "said Cathleen.

"What do you mean? You're husband is nothing but a lazy lout," retorted Edie.

"Why you . . ."

The head nurse hurried over. She knelt on one knee and spoke quietly. As she finished, she said firmly, "So I want you both to try and get along."

Cathleen plaintively asked, "Try to get a long what?"

This true gem was contributed by my friend, Lynne, a nurse.

Dottie O

"They call me Dottie O," she told me when I introduced myself to her.

I met Dottie five years ago when I visited my Dad at the nursing home. She usually greeted me in the hallway where she sat with three other ladies.

There was a special gathering one Christmas time where family members and residents shared holiday memories. Dottie's favorite memories were times spent with her sons and their wives and children. Her toothless smile broadened whenever she talked about her family.

Dottie caught my attention, not because she was loud or funny; it was her serenity that got to me.

Recently, I read in the paper that a woman named Dorothy O'Leary passed away at the home. Even though I supposed Dottie was in her nineties, her passing made me sad.

When I next visited the home to meet with some of the folks for coffee, I spotted a woman wheeling herself down to the activities room. I was drawn to her thinning hair and the long, single braid hanging slightly over the back of her wheelchair.

I quickened my pace, and as I got beside her, saw that it was Dottie O!

"Good morning. I'm so glad to see you," I told her, as I quickly brushed away my happy tears. She had *no idea* just how glad I was to see her.

I still don't know her last name, but I'm happy it is not O'Leary.

Carol and Peter

*C*arol and Peter lived together for thirty years before moving into the nursing home. Peter is a sweet, quiet man who mostly does as the nagging Carol orders.

He is an avid reader, and I suspect he enjoys a certain amount of peace by escaping into the pages of his books.

Carol enjoys dressing up and being the boss lady.

"Peter, clean off your tray. Breakfast is coming." Or, "Hurry up in the bathroom so I can get in there." On and on throughout the day, the routine is the same.

I often wonder how this long-suffering man puts up with her.

Carol surprises me one morning, though, as we head to the bathroom to get her washed up and ready for the day. She likes sleeping in a Johnny and when Peter glances up to say "good morning" to me, Carol flips one side of the Johnny, stops in her tracks, looks at Peter and says, "Eat your heart out, Peter!" Then she gives me a grin and a wink.

One terrible day, Peter gets sick; too sick to recover. Carol never leaves his side during the last few days of his life. She holds his hand, brushes his white hair from his feverish brow and speaks softly to "the best friend I ever had."

I think the woman who displayed her gruff side was all show.

Mildred

I enjoy visiting a small group of ladies who live in a nearby nursing home. Mildred, one of my favorites, has not yet come down for this morning's coffee klatch.

When I get to the East Wing to bring her down in her wheel chair, I see there are no nurses at the desk. There is one nurse at the end of the hall manning the med cart. Two call lights are on, one of which is over Mildred's doorway. I am dismayed there are no aides in sight anywhere.

I enter Mildred's room and find her still in bed, under a mess of blankets hanging every which way in a heap. The room reeks of urine. It is almost 10 o'clock

"Good morning, Mildred. Are you sick today?"

"No, I'm not sick. No one got me up yet."

It is Saturday, and I know from personal experience that the nurses' aides are always short-handed on the weekend. Mildred requires two people to assist her with a Hoyer lift to move her from her bed and get her ready for the day.

As cheerfully as I can, I tell her, "If you don't make it down to coffee hour, I will come back and share with you what you missed."

She thanks me, and I'm sure we're both thinking the same thing: *she will not be joining the group this morning.*

I return to East Wing an hour later. Everything is the same. My friend's call light is still on and the nurse with the med cart is standing in the same place she was in the first time I passed her. No one else is around at all.

Mildred is glad to see me. She asks, "Please get someone. I need my oxygen."

I go to the nurse with this request and she comes immediately to Mildred's room and gives her the oxygen. When Mildred asks to get up, the nurse tells her, in drippy sweetness as though my friend is an imbecile, "Not now, honey. It's almost time for your lunch. We don't want you to miss lunch. Okay, honey?"

Mildred nods and says, "Okay, I'll wait."

At this point, I'm wishing inside I knew how to fix the system and make a difference. The state visits once or twice a year to observe that all is well in its facilities, but the staffing never improves. Nothing seems to change for these beautiful old treasures and the caring people who work here and love them.

When the nurse leaves the room, I ask Mildred if she is up to hearing about the coffee hour.

"Oh, yes!" she answers gladly.

After I share what has gone on with the group, this dear lady tells me, "You are such a wonderful person. I always enjoy your company."

I hug her goodbye and, as I walk down the hall, I wonder if I will be as accepting and gracious when *my* turn comes to live in a nursing home.

Anna

As I and several co-workers drink our coffee in the break room before our 7 a.m. shift begins, Anna is already walking the hallways, checking out the goings on and reporting them to us with great authority. She has lived here at the nursing home longer than anyone.

On this particular morning, she observes what is taking place behind the closed doors of the activities room where the department heads are meeting.

"Hey! They're talkin' about new drapes. They're gonna have some company make 'em. They could get the same thing at WalMart, but they're not gonna *do* it. It's gonna cost a lot of money. You'll see." She turns and continues down the hallway to her room, grumbling to herself.

We nurses' aides get a kick out of Anna's imagination, until about six weeks later, when we arrive for work to find new, custom-made drapes hanging to match the new couches and chairs that grace the sitting room.

At lunchtime we notice the chairs have been reupholstered to match the new draperies hanging in the dining room.

I wonder if Anna knows when the staff will meet to discuss how much our raises will be. If we're lucky, some of us may notice her grumbling early on another morning when the department heads meet again.

Dee Dee

*D*ee Dee loved saying my name. She quickly became my buddy as she was bossy, sweet and feisty. Although tiny and nearly blind, she took charge of her wants and needs.

"I'm going to wear those soft, blue pants with my white sweater today." Then sweetly, "Okay, Eunice?"

"I want to drink my coffee after you put me in my chair."

"Eunice, you have to put my panties the other way," she told me when I first began taking care of her.

I said, "They are already frontwards."

"No, no! Turn them around," she instructed firmly.

"You mean inside out?" I asked.

"Yes, Eunice", was her matter-of-fact answer.

"The same goes for my slacks, shirt and sweater, too. Oh yes, my socks, too, Eunice."

"Dee Dee, why do you want to wear everything inside out? Is this for good luck or something?" I wanted to know.

She smiled and said, "Yes, for good luck."

One of the other nurses' aides who had been in this business far longer than I, explained Dee Dee's way prevented the seams from digging into her delicate skin.

This little lady was a whiner much of the time, but she was so darned cute, I couldn't be angry with her. When she saw me, she'd holler, "Eunice, I didn't get hand lotion on me this morning" or "Eunice, my tea was cold at breakfast and nobody would warm it up for me."

Her roommate's husband Richard visited every day at lunchtime. When Dee Dee continued her list of complaints, Richard would say, "No, that's not true. The girls do what you ask them to do."

With a sad, pouty face, Dee Dee insisted softly, in her little-girl voice, "No they don't, Eunice." These moments just made me *have* to hug her and pat her back, *as* I winked over her shoulder at Richard.

Alice

*A*lice, number three of eleven children, lives in a retirement home. Although elderly, she is still beautiful and loves to sing the songs she writes. Every time I visit her, she is happy, smiling, and often singing. Alice always wears hats she has designed. My favorite is the beige straw one, with its brim turned up all around, a large yellow flower pinned slightly to the right of her pretty face.

Today, when I visit her, she greets me with her usual good-natured smile and tells me, "I want to read you this letter I got from my son. He wasn't what you would call *a good boy.* He sold drugs and took drugs. He's in jail now."

She unfolds the letter and begins to read.

"Dear Mom, I hope you are doing well. I am hanging in okay and will be out in three months. Please be there for me as I need your moral support when I get out of here."

As she looks up at me, I tell her, "See, he still needs his mom."

Alice, pointing to her heart, says, "And I still need him, too."

She carefully re-folds the note and places it into her small purse.

We nod our mutual understanding as we hide our trials from the world.

Birdie

Although Birdie is in her nineties, her skin is as clear and wrinkle free as a young girl's.

A stroke has left her with a speech impediment, but she is sweet and soft spoken. Her shapely legs no longer move. As I dress her, I imagine how she could have been a ballerina or a member of the Rockettes years ago.

After placing her in the Hoyer Lift, I transfer her to a wheelchair. I love brushing her cloud-white hair. It is like forming shapes out of whipped cream.

She loves having lotion applied to her paralyzed hands before I take her down to the lobby to join the other residents.

Birdie is the most beautiful old angel I have ever seen.

Diane

The most interesting resident I knew was Diane. She had a private room and shared much of her life, past and present with me. I learned a great deal from this woman, who was in her late eighties when we met.

At first glance, her appearance could be described as "gross". She was skinny rather than thin, had a hump back from osteoporosis, and the worst blotchy and blue-veined skin I had ever seen. Her long, dry salt and pepper hair made her face look shrunken. Diane always wore nail polish, deep pink, on her too-long fingernails.

Luckily, I did not scare easily, because as I got to know her, Diane taught me a very valuable lesson. She loved herself without vanity or shame.

Her clothes were fancy and colorful, and choosing jewelry for the day took at least ten minutes. She surprised me one morning by confiding she had made an appointment for cosmetic surgery. I could not imagine her surviving all those hours under anesthesia!

"I am going to have the tear in my earlobe repaired. My skin is so thin now, this is the second time the weight of my earring caused the tear", she explained.

She returned from the day surgery elated and anxious to wear her sapphire earrings once again as soon as she healed.

Since we had become friends, I shared some of my personal life with her. When I told her I had divorced my husband after almost thirty-two years of marriage, she shared her divorce experience with me, too.

"I divorced my husband after forty years because I couldn't take his swearing any more" she told me. "I later wanted to take him back, but he said, 'no'."

When poor health made it impossible for her to remain in her home, she moved into the nursing home. Since meeting me, she begged me to move into her house and become her twenty-four/seven caregiver. She reasoned it was a good idea because I would not have to pay any rent. Salary was never mentioned. I thanked her for the offer, but explained I needed to live in my own home as I had children and friends and did not want to move.

After several months passed, I shared with Diane the happy news I had met the divorced man who moved into the apartment next door to mine. She loved hearing about my going dancing with this fellow and how we laughed together and how happy we were.

Months later, I was unable to hide my sad news from her that "Mr. Wonderful" was going back to his ex-wife.

The day after I shared my heartache with her, she asked one of the aides to have me come to her room. When I got there, she asked me for my former boyfriend's last name and address. "I will write you a character reference and send it to him", she told me earnestly. I was both amused and touched by this wonderful gesture of friendship.

I assured her I would be okay, although it would take me a while to move on.

Eventually, Diane made the decision to move on as well and gave up her dream of moving back to her house.

Her former home was to be auctioned off and her friend came to pick her up to see it happen.

Diane passed away the following day. I think she died from a broken heart.

Brotherly Love

$\mathcal{I}$ dial Gene's telephone so he can speak to his sister Blanche. As always, she is happy to hear from him.

They each live in Florida nursing homes, but are hours apart in location.

Gene, ninety-five years young, is easy going, takes life as it comes, and is content "as long as there is no pain."

Blanche, ninety-seven, takes the opposite approach to life. She wants to be back in her house, even though she is unable to care for herself there. Since moving to the nursing home, she keeps to herself as she does not like being surrounded by "all of these strangers."

Gene, tells her, "Go out and make friends with the people and they won't be strangers anymore."

"I would just like to meet a man in a tuxedo who will take me to a nice restaurant where we could have a romantic, candlelit dinner once in a while."

In true, brotherly fashion, Gene says, "That's not gonna happen, Blanche. Forget that stuff."

Blanche is crying now. "Why should I give up my dream?" she asks him.

"Because they're all *dead,* Blanche."

When she hangs up on him, he turns to me, baffled, and says, "What the hell is the matter with *her*?"

Eunice

$\mathcal{W}$e bond even before we meet, as she and I have the same, unusual, first name.

Eunice's things arrive the day before she moves into her private room at the nursing home.

I am assigned the task of setting up her room, hanging her clothes in the closet, and arranging her belongings into the drawers of the dresser she brings from home.

As I place her dainty perfume bottles on the mirrored tray on top of her dresser, I cannot resist unscrewing the silver cap from a familiar-looking dark blue bottle and taking a whiff. *Evening in Paris* instantly brings back memories of getting ready for the Mount Carmel dances when I am in the tenth grade. I cannot wait to meet this woman.

On the morning of her arrival, I am surprised to see how frail my namesake is. She is very thin and has to be on oxygen around the clock.

Since she has a private room and stays by herself most of the time, I like visiting with her. We have some interesting conversations about religion, politics and life in general. One really great revelation is, she dated "Dr. Seuss" a few times and tells me, "He was very charming."

She, too, wore *Evening in Paris* perfume when she went dancing years ago, just as I had. Now that her lungs are weak, she no longer wears perfume, but enjoys "the pretty bottles."

Eunice has a very sweet disposition as does her daughter who visits every day at lunchtime to make sure her mother eats at least half of her meal.

As I watch them sitting side by side most afternoons, I wonder, when my time comes to be in a nursing home, if my daughter and I will replay this scene.

Ed

*I*f Ed had been a dog instead of a man, he would have been a Basset Hound. He was sad and whiney, but generous. I liked him. Every day that I took care of him, he told me to help myself to the candy he kept in his drawer.

Ed never wanted to get ready for breakfast, and tried to talk me into letting him stay in his bed. No matter how hard I worked to engage him in pleasant conversation, he complained about being stuck in a nursing home instead of living with his daughter, or not being able to do anything by himself without needing help. One of his major problems was, he didn't even attempt to help himself.

Every now and then, I got a glimpse of the man he had been before circumstances and poor health changed him.

He shared with me what his life had been like before he moved into the nursing home. Ed had been married twice and was very close to his daughter Eileen from his first marriage. His second wife was his "favorite" and he was very sad about her having died four years earlier.

Since two months had passed and he never did settle in, his daughter decided to bring him home to Florida to live with her. I wondered if she had any idea what a full-time job it would be for her to care for her father.

The day I got him ready to move from New Hampshire, he told me, "I'll never forget you, Honey, because you are my friend." I was very touched by his words.

We received the sad news that he passed away the week after leaving us.

Ed, I know you're up there somewhere and want you to know I will never forget you, either. I hope you are enjoying time with your second wife.

Running Hot and Cold

*O*ne of the things I observed pretty early on as a nurses' aide in a nursing home, was how cold old people's skin is despite the temperature of the room. Perhaps inactivity causes this phenomenon.

Working there had me running most of the day, so my hands were always warm

My facility was not equipped with air conditioning and I longed to open the windows during the summer on less humid days. The usual response from most of the residents was, "That wind is cold. Close the window!" This order was sometimes followed by a request to "get my sweater, please."

Perhaps their skin was so cold because they are closer to death than they are to life.

One day, as I reached out to take her hand, poor Carla accused loudly, "You *burned* me!" as she quickly removed her cold hand from my hot one.

Still having hot flashes at sixty, hopefully is a sign I still have a long way to go!

Gloria

A dozen residents are gathered in the Day Room to hear Ellen, the singer/guitar player.

In her soft, church-lady voice, Ellen attempts to encourage the folks to join her in "Daisy, Daisy, give me your answer, do . . ." Eugene complies, but he's the only one. Some of the men and women just sit quietly while others nod off to sleep.

Gloria, the lady seated in the recliner chair in the corner, pipes up. "Play my favorite one."

"I will play it last," Ellen assures her. "I won't forget."

After a few bars of, *"Heart of my Heart, Swing Low Sweet Chariot, East Side West Side* and *Take me out to the Ballgame"*, Gloria asks again, "Is it time for my favorite song yet?"

Debbie, the Activities Director signals Ellen it is time to move on to another wing of the facility.

"Here we go, Gloria. It's time for your song", Ellen announces.

To my delight and surprise, Ellen belts out James Brown's "I Feel Good" as Gloria waves her arms up over her head, a smile of satisfaction lighting up her beautiful, wrinkled face.

Alan

The twinkle in Alan's eye sends a message that he was, and still is, a ladies' man. He wears a boyish smile that belies his ninety-four years. My personal favorite description, "cute as a button" fits him perfectly. He strikes me as the sort of fellow who probably got into trouble in school for dipping a little girl's pigtails into the inkwell, or making a classmate laugh out loud when the teacher's back was turned.

He always greets me with a cheery, "Hello there, honey", a wink, and if he were close enough, a pat just below my waist. I answer back with a smile, "Hello there, Alan", as I move his hand up a little higher and wink back at him!

Alan uses a walker, but he and I play a game every now and then when the nurse's back is turned. I whisper, "Hey Alan! Wanna dance?" Moving the walker to the side, we join hands, move our feet side to side as my "partner" sings, ending with a wonderful yodel! The yodel *always* ends the dance as the nurse can't help hearing it!

Our game is short, safe and lots of fun for both of us; not so much for the resident ladies in the lobby, who glare at Alan, yelling for him to *shut up*. We have to steer clear of Iona who swings her walker at him whenever he sings.

I see a sweet and lively old man, but his peer group, I suppose, sees something quite different.

Helen

*H*elen, nearly blind, stays actively connected to the world.

She listens to books on tape, supplied by Sight Services, an agency that lends a special machine and audio books to blind or handicapped people.

Every morning, she takes several minutes to decide which outfit to wear. This makes me nervous, as I am allotted just a short amount of time to ready each resident for the day.

Shower days are especially time consuming. Helen has her own shampoo, conditioner, and routine. Her hair has to be shampooed twice with a thorough rinsing before the conditioner is applied. She cannot stand, so she insists on being dried while seated in the shower chair, then covered with a different, larger bath towel and taken back to her room to be dressed. All the other residents are dressed in the shower room before being taken back to their rooms.

Once in her room, Helen applies her special cream to her face. She has a special cream for her feet, too, which must be applied with a five-minute foot rub.

She brushes and styles her own hair while I dry it, swishing the nozzle of the hair dryer back and forth ever so slowly. This lady enjoys being pampered.

She loves to talk the entire time, too. Helen is an interesting woman who shares family stories and current events with me. I wish I could spend more, unrushed time with this ninety-six year old jewel.

In a roundabout way, I *am* still spending unrushed time with Helen as she was instrumental in finding my dream home for me a year after my divorce.

My realtor Maureen showed me many small houses, mobile homes, and town houses. As we got to know one another, she shared that her grandmother was a resident in the nursing home where I worked. I was delighted to learn Helen was her grandmother.

"I know just the right place for you, Maureen told me one afternoon. You are well suited for a garden condo."

As soon as we walked into the place, I knew I was home.

I credit Helen with being my "Home-Finding Angel". She will be with me as long as I live here in my very own little piece of paradise.

Lana

"Two pinks and a white", she tells us earnestly every morning as we roll the breakfast trolley down the hall towards her room.

We'd squeeze by her wheel chair where she sits waiting in her doorway. As we place the tray of juice, oatmeal, and coffee on her bedside table, she keeps reminding us, "two pinks and a white."

And every morning as we leave her room, she pats her two packets of Sweet and Low and the packet of sugar, saying softly to herself, "two pinks and a white. She then looks up at us, beaming her one-toothed smile, nodding her head in satisfaction.

Happily, for all concerned, serenity is once again restored; until Lana hears the lunch cart coming down the hallway.

We serve lunch to the chant, "Two pinks and a white" coming from the doorway of 40 West.

Raymond

Raymond is frail, his face gaunt, his eyes cloudy, but his voice belies his wasted physical appearance.

Most of the nurses and aides think of him as a crusty old geezer, but I like him because he is "real"; kind of "honest to a fault." Whatever he is thinking just shoots out of his mouth like a loose cannonball. I find him, well, *interesting.* Blameless, too, because he *is* pretty old. He makes me laugh so hard inside myself some days, I can't wait to get *outside*, just to let the chuckles out.

One afternoon, as he and I take a stroll down the hallway, he stops abruptly, plants his walker firmly in front of him and glances into the room of two female residents.

"*Look* at 'em. Just a couple of old hags," he bellows, shaking his head in disgust.

Next doorway, same thing. He grimaces, showing his yellowed upper denture.

"*That* one looks half *dead*," he remarks about a woman asleep in her wheelchair in the hallway.

"Raymond, your remarks are unkind," I tell him.

"I tell it like I see it", retorts my grouchy buddy.

At the end of our walk on this day, I am left with wonder and gratitude.

I wonder if Raymond owns a mirror.

I'm grateful all these women are *very* hard of hearing.

Lois

Lois is not as sociable as some of the other residents, but she is always pleasant when I come to her room to take care of her for the day.

She is a bit off balance, even with the aid of a cane. Sometimes I wonder if she had been tipsy before she moved into the nursing home. The blood vessels under her skin make her nose perpetually red and she seems a little "off" much of the time, perhaps due to her diabetes.

She complains many times a day, "I didn't have any breakfast," although she eats everything on her plate at every meal. The scale proves, every week that this woman is far from starving.

One morning, as I help Lois wash herself, she holds up her hand and tells me, "Look! I must be getting fat."

"Why do you say that, Lois?"

"Because the girl who helped me get ready for bed last night couldn't get my ring off my finger."

"Why did she want to take your ring off?"

"She said it was real pretty and wanted to try it on. She even tried soap, but it wouldn't come off."

Alarmed, I report this to the charge nurse, who says, "Oh, Lois is confused. I'm sure nothing like that happened."

Lois' diamond is huge and beautiful; I believe her.

When I take my break, I phone my friend Diane who works second shift, and tell her what my resident has shared. Sure enough, someone was on duty the night before from an agency we had not used before. My friend becomes my spy.

She informs me the following day that this person has not been on duty the second night. I give the charge nurse a "head's up", to make sure this person will not return to our facility. There is no proof she had done anything, but my gut feeling tells me to believe my confused resident.

Maude

*E*ighty-seven year old Maude likes hanging out near the nurses' station. She sits in her wheelchair busily knitting, but she's also listening to "nurses' talk". The highlight of her day is sharing her knowledge of medical jargon with some of the other residents.

I am here every day at the nursing home visiting a family member. As he is being tended to by a physical therapist on this particular day, I am pretending to read a magazine in the day room. What I am really doing is eavesdropping on Maude's conversation.

She is explaining to the woman seated next to her that someone on this wing is having an "in-tes-**tinal** problem" and the nurse is waiting for a call from the doctor on how to treat this condition.

Maude hopes the doctor on call is the one who helped diagnose her *very close veins*

Grace

She sits in her wheel chair at the four corners, where the East and West wings cross. The twinkle in her eyes is hidden behind her round dark eyeglass frames. At first glance, Grace is a serious-looking woman with her painted brown eyebrows hanging like horizontal parentheses over her glasses. Her four lady friends sit with her, but usually only get to say "hello" to visitors. The other ladies play second fiddle to the self-appointed spokeswoman for the group. Grace's daily greeting, "Hi, Hon" makes everyone feel at ease when they enter the nursing home to visit.

A well-meaning volunteer, attempting to get to know her, gets a surprise when she asks, "Tell me something about yourself, dear."

Grace's quick wit kicks in when she replies, "I'm three months pregnant with Chuck Norris' baby. What else do you want to know?"

Momentarily taken aback, the volunteer laughs and says, "I'll never forget *your* name."

"It's Veronica Lake," the eighty-something year old, wise-cracking great-grandma replies.

Maddie

*M*addie suffered a stroke and was very obese, making it necessary for her to move out of her home. Her body remained paralyzed on one side and she was unable to stand because of her excessive weight.

It was difficult to wash and dress her without another team member helping to turn her. I dreaded having her on my list for the week as I had to really work at getting her ready for the day. Two aides were required to get her out of bed and back into it. I was more than grateful when a couple of good team members were scheduled on my shift, as I only weighed ninety-seven pounds and needed all the help I could get.

Maddie's favorite pastime was eating and watching soap operas on TV. A couple of her friends sneaked in candy and cookies. She tried to bribe me into buying doughnuts for her, but I managed to squirm my way out of that request.

She was a sweet lady who volunteered to be the guinea pig when our nurses-aide instructor needed to teach us a skill by demonstrating on a resident. Thanks to Maddie's generosity, we learned how to brush dentures, cut fingernails, properly bathe someone in bed, change a bed with someone in it, perform a backrub, change a diaper, and engage someone, whether they were able to respond or not. She even allowed us to learn how to care for her colostomy, which I named her "badge of courage". We learned all of these things in our certified nursing assistant course, but hands-on training with a living, breathing resident was a priceless experience.

I will never forget this woman's willingness to allow us to "practice" on her.

On a friendship level, I spent many hours visiting with her after work. She and I were close in age and shared stories about our lives outside the nursing home.

As tough as it was taking care of her physical needs, I would not have missed the opportunity to have known her. Maddie was a blessing.

Uncle Eddie

Uncle Eddie lives in Connecticut near the home he shared with his daughter, my cousin Wendy, until a few months ago.

No longer safe at home while Wendy is at work, Uncle Eddie has been moved to a medium-sized, cheerful nursing home. He has settled in very well, to the relief of his two daughters.

My cousin Joan lives in Illinois and calls her father every Sunday to see how he is getting along.

There is no answer on this January first afternoon when she calls to wish him "Happy new year".

Joan redials and reaches the nurses' desk. She is relieved to learn Wendy has taken their dad to his favorite Chinese restaurant.

When Joan phones him the next day, Uncle Eddie tells of the wonderful time he has had "at Wendy's house", where she cooked him "all kinds of food."

Amused by his mild confusion about the restaurant, Joan asks what his plans are for today. "Oh," he answers, "I have already walked ten miles on the treadmill this morning."

"Really Dad? You've walked *ten miles*?"

"Oh sure", says Eddie. "You can do just about anything you set your mind to."

My ninety-six year old uncle has innocently placed a positive spin on memory and aging.

Wally

The east wing of the nursing facility is filled with a lively bunch of seniors this Sunday morning.

Hope, the young nurse, is at her cart preparing the medications for her residents.

As Wally gets up from his wheel chair, the alarm that is clipped to his shirt comes undone from his wheelchair handle and begins sounding its loud chirp.

Hope turns around and says sharply, "Sit down, Wally!"

"I don't *want* to sit down," he tells her.

Doris, whose eyes are mostly closed, states quietly from her recliner chair, "I don't want to sit down either."

Hope sits Wally back down at the table and reminds him he has a pile of newspapers to read.

He shouts, "I don't *want* to read the damn papers!"

Doris parrots softly, "I don't want to read the papers either.

Lorraine, who rarely speaks, tells Hope *she* doesn't want the papers.

Hope, clearly frustrated now, scoops the Sunday newspapers up and slams them onto a nearby table.

"*There*. Now just be patient. It's almost lunchtime."

Wally gets up again and declares, "I'm sick of sitting in the damn chair. I want to take a *walk*."

As he teeters away from the wheelchair with the alarm screaming again, he orders the nurse to "turn that damn thing off!"

She says, "If you sit at the table, I'll bring you an ice cream. Would you like that?"

He says, "Okay," as Doris tells no one in particular, "I want an ice cream, too."

An amused family member remarks to Hope, "I'll bet *you'd* love a *drink*."

The nurse smiles, nodding.

As the visitor departs, Doris is saying, "*I'd* love a drink, too."

Ruthie

She had lived here at the retirement home longer than everyone and knows *everything* about *anything* that went on around the place. If she hadn't been a resident of this facility, she would certainly have qualified to be the boss.

Ruthie was less than five feet tall with tiny hands, and tiny feet that headed towards one another as she walked down the hallways while she held onto the railings. Her enormous breasts, hanging over her waistband, swung from side to side and her mouth kept busy constantly as she chewed her tongue.

She especially liked telling me how to do my job, as I was the greenest nurses' aide on staff when Ruthie and I met.

As I tried very hard to help her with her morning ritual of washing herself and helping her get dressed, she kept me on edge the whole time I was with her. "Honey", she'd say, "I don't mean to give ya a hard time or nothin' . . . .", then stop in mid sentence and shake her head. She did very well in conveying the message to me that I was the dumbest thing she had encountered in a very long time.

After I had been put through my paces with her, Ruthie would tell me, "Don't worry, honey. You're doin' a good job."

One day as she was seated in the lobby and I was heading down the hall to answer a call bell, Ruthie grabbed my arm. "Honey," she told me, "Somebody's dead in the room at the end."

How sad, I thought, how the elderly sometimes have fears like children do. I tried to reassure Ruthie. "No one is dead, dear. Everything is all right."

She rolled her eyes and shook her head as I went on my way down the hallway.

When I headed to the last room with a cup of juice, I gently touched the little lady's shoulder as she sat napping in her wheelchair. No response. I felt for a pulse; nothing.

As I came up to inform the nurse at the front desk in as calm a demeanor as I could muster, Ruthie said as I passed her, "See, I *told* ya she was dead."

Ah, Ruthie was a real trip!

The Haitian Nursing Assistant

The catastrophic earthquake that hit Haiti in 2010 touched me because I knew a few Haitian nurses' aides during my time as a caregiver. They were kind, gentle and spiritual women.

On one occasion, when I was a certified nursing assistant, I was asked by a resident's family member to do a "one on one" nightshift. They did not want their dying relative Arlene to be alone.

I knew and loved Arlene and was happy to stay with her. What a harrowing, sleepless night it turned out to be. This poor little lady was restless and wanted to keep getting up to use the bathroom. She kept requesting something cold to drink and wanted me to hold her hand, "even after I'm asleep."

When a Haitian aide came to relieve me the next morning, I informed her of Arlene's passing a short time before her arrival.

The replacement aide looked at Arlene, and placed both of her hands in the dead woman's hands. She then walked over to the window, raising it wide open, and waved her arms.

Startled, I stood, wary, with my eyebrows raised.

The kind woman quietly explained: "I was letting her spirit go free."

Warm Fuzzies

I meet with residents of a local nursing home about once a month to share memories and enjoy their company.

Since I am a senior citizen myself, I feel comfortable acknowledging how different life is for them, from before they came to live here. I feel it is also important to remind them how lovely it is to have made so many new friends in our age group. This is why I come up with the idea to share *warm fuzzies*, a few words highlighting good memories of things or people that make us feel happy. A warm fuzzy can be our children, chocolate, flowers; whatever puts a smile on our faces.

We fill out our words on strips of paper, fold them and place them into our metal "Warm Fuzzy Chest" every month. We will read them at the end of the year to remind ourselves of all the things we are grateful for. The men and women like the idea.

What fun this is! One fellow says his warm fuzzy is "a gin and tonic on the deck. "That always makes me warm and fuzzy", he shares with a laugh.

"I love being able to get out of my bed and walk around", Mary tells the group, while the others at the table nod in agreement.

"Joyce, do you have a warm fuzzy to add?" I ask.

"Yes, I love when my granddaughter brings her little baby to see me."

Most folks share they love being with their families; others tell about their favorite cat or dog; still others mention favorite ice-cream flavors.

I am startled when Lila, a very pleasant woman, shares *her* warm fuzzy: "Mind your business!"

"Lila, that doesn't sound like a warm fuzzy to me", I tell her.

"Sure it is! If everyone would mind their own business, everyone else would be happier, and that's a warm fuzzy to me!"

This smart observation comes from a woman who has Alzheimer's disease.

There's a lot of wisdom floating around this place. That's what keeps me coming back.

Betsy

*B*etsy is another of my favorite residents where I am an aide at a nursing home.

She is a large Polish lady with big, puffy white hair and sparkling blue eyes. Betsy exhibits the familiar sarcasm I grew up with in my own Polish family, which I enjoy tremendously. She is all attitude in the way she sometimes laughs, more like a "*huh*" without the grin, unless she is laughing at her own jokes; then her laughter is pure merriment.

In the morning, when I get her up into her stuffed chair, she energetically begins her own kind of exercise by singing, "Y.M.C.A.", while giving her arms a good stretch.

The nursing staff becomes concerned when Betsy begins refusing to eat her meals. I ask her why she doesn't touch her food. She has a perfectly valid explanation.

"Because the food here tastes like *shit*! I was a good cook when I lived at home. Nobody knows how to cook around here."

Betsy maintains her weight by enjoying the stash of doughnuts she keeps in a plastic container in her closet. I'm pretty sure her daughter is unaware these treats are her mom's main diet. I have no intention of squealing because I can relate. I have a sweet tooth, too.

She isn't really bossy, but Betsy certainly does as she wishes. This woman never allows me to help her into bed as I had been taught to do in my certified nurses' training class. She faces her bed with her back to me, and orders me with one word: "*GO!*"

This means I am to push her butt as she leans forward. Betsy then proceeds to crawl to the far edge of her bed and then push on the wall to get the momentum to land on her back.

As the months pass, Betsy gets it into her head that she has a cat. After breakfast, she saves part of her oatmeal for "the kitty". I place the bowl under her bed every morning for weeks, removing it when Betsy is in the bathroom.

One morning when I get to work, I am told Betsy has been taken to the hospital during the night.

Later that morning, Ellen, one of the housekeepers asks, as I place a bowl of oatmeal under the bed, "What are you doing?"

"Feeding Betsy's cat", I answer.

Suddenly, I realize I will probably be moving in here before too long.

SECTION TWO
Other Unique Seniors

Aunt Gertrude

*A*unt Gertrude, my mother's oldest sister, was my godmother. My aunt had pretty, short blonde hair, light blue eyes, and straight beautiful teeth. Her laugh made me laugh.

She took me to Florida on a train to meet another of her sisters, my Aunt Val when I was about three years old. My big memory of that trip was the exciting time I had on the train leading all the way to Tampa. Our bed was the top berth behind a curtain where I sat in the middle of the night eating vanilla snap cookies out of the box while Aunt Gertrude slept. It was fun having my very own picnic while looking out the window at all the houses and trees whizzing by along the tracks.

She told the porter how worried she was about me because I never ate anything when we went to the dining car. She didn't make a big fuss about me, though, the way my father's sisters did.

Aunt Gertrude didn't have any children and she lived in a high-rise apartment in New York City with my Uncle Archie, who looked like Clark Gable because of his mustache. I didn't get to see them too much because the rest of our family lived in houses in New Jersey.

I remember visiting the New York apartment a couple of times with my father. My dad told me Aunt Gertrude cooked the best steak in her broiler and she served delicious food on beautiful dishes.

I loved to listen to her talk because she still had a little bit of her Polish ("excent") accent. Uncle Archie smiled a lot while Aunt Gertrude talked. I was still young when my uncle died.

My aunt sewed me many beautiful dresses when I was a little girl. After my mother died and Dad remarried, I hardly ever saw her, but we wrote letters back and forth. I met her second husband Connie a few times and liked him very much.

When I was nineteen, Aunt Gertrude sent me a letter my mother had written from her hospital bed when I was a baby. She kept it all those years to give to me after I moved out of my stepmother's house so this cherished letter wouldn't be destroyed.

A few years after Uncle Connie died, Aunt Gertrude married Tony, another very nice man. By then, Aunt Gertrude was older and sold her apartment and moved to Tampa, Florida with her new, and last, husband.

She and Tony came to visit us when my two boys, Bobby and Michael were three and two years old. Aunt Gertrude was in her late sixties by then and had as much pep and energy as I did. After putting on her tailored pajamas, she invited my boys to exercise with her on my living-room floor; they were delighted! She kept popping in and out of the bathroom while she brushed her teeth, checking on what the kids were up to.

When I told her she and Tony would be sleeping in my bed, she said, "Thank you, Honey, but I have some good advice for you and never forget this. Don't ever give up your bed for anybody, not even the pope!" I never saw her after that visit, but we wrote letters to one another on a regular basis.

She mailed me a check every year at Christmas time with a note to "buy the children Carter's pajamas."

My cousin Joanie was closer to Aunt Gertrude as her mom was Gertrude's baby sister. Joanie's son and daughter had a very different experience than my sons had when they first met Aunt Gertrude.

As Joanie tells the story: "The first time she met my kids, she breezed into my house and announced 'Hi, I'm your Aunt Gertrude' as she whipped off her wig and, waving it, said, 'This is my prosteshe' (Polish word for wig)!"

"I don't think my poor Laurie was ever the same after that meeting," Joanie told me.

Aunt Gertrude survived two brothers, three sisters and three husbands, living a pretty active life for over ninety years.

Although I had not spent as much time with Aunt Gertrude as I had with my other aunts, she was like my very own "Auntie Mame", leaving fairy dust in her wake as only a godmother can.

The Local Farm

*O*ur new town in New Hampshire was much more rural than the Connecticut one we left behind in November of 1975.

The first year we lived there, we decided to plant a vegetable garden. All of our neighbors got their manure from Johnson's Farm and suggested we take a ride over.

We loaded two galvanized garbage barrels and a shovel into the back of our pickup truck and drove the mile and a half to the farm.

The farmland boasted many acres and local travelers often had to sit in bumper to bumper traffic while a line of runaway cows ventured across the street towards The Country Store. Soon, old Farmer Johnson would come along to herd the girls back to their home turf.

What a bargain Mr. Johnson gave us. Year after year, off we trekked to the farm for our fifty-cent fertilizer.

One day we were in for a shock. *Mrs.* Johnson came out of her house to greet us. When we told her why we were there, she motioned us to where we could help ourselves. The woman stood watching, with her hands on her hips until we had shoveled in the last load.

We soon realized, not only was she the farmer's wife, she was also a shrewd business woman, charging us double the going rate!

Tracing the Family Tree—Short Version

*F*or as long as I can remember, I have been told my mother's parents were born in Poland. My father's mother was born in Poland. My father's father was "three-quarters Polish and one-quarter Russian."

Fast forward sixty-nine years to when my cousin Louise decides to trace our ancestry. We are hoping for some great revelations about who we are. Our maiden name doesn't sound Polish at all, even when we spell it the way our grandfather spelled it back in the old country.

I am very drawn to all things Italian; my cousin Brenda is drawn to Greece and visits there often. Many of the Polish words my grandmother speaks when I am a little girl turn out to be Yiddish. My cousins and I wait anxiously for the DNA results to unlock the mysteries of our family.

When Louise tells our only surviving aunt, my father's sister, that we are waiting for exciting news about our ancestry, this is what she says:

"Don't waste your money. I can fill in the blanks. We have Italian mixture in our blood."

Surprised, Louise asks, "How do you know?"

Auntie replies, "Because your grandfather had an affair with an Italian woman."

Aunt Jennie

Aunt Jennie, my father's baby sister, is my only living aunt. Her eighty-ninth birthday is coming up soon. Still feisty and young at heart, she is frustrated about being physically off balance, even when she uses her walker. She has a number of health problems and her late husband, my Uncle Ted, had been taking wonderful care of her for years.

Their daughter Lenore never married and lived upstairs in her parents' two family home. Her brother Gordon lived two hours away with his wife and two children. Aunt Jennie and Uncle Ted counted on Lenore to prepare supper when she got home from her full-time job and take them to their medical appointments which were scheduled around her work hours.

Three days before last Christmas, Lenore was rushed to the hospital by ambulance where she died four days later. Her loss was a great shock to the family.

Cousin Gordon now had the job of caring for his parents. He and his wife Ginny started building an addition onto their home. The plan was for Aunt Jennie and Uncle Ted to be close by in their new in-law apartment instead of two hours away. They were due to move in around June or July.

Five months after Lenore's death, Uncle Ted was taken to the hospital with breathing problems. The family learned that he had lung cancer. He passed away four hours later.

Since the addition was not yet finished, Gordon hired a live-in companion to stay with Aunt Jennie in her own home. Gordon and Ginny stayed at Aunt Jennie's for the next five weekends.

When Aunt Jennie found herself alone after Uncle Ted died and struggling with a number of health problems, her son set up an interview with a woman from an assisted-living facility.

Colorful brochures showed my aunt how lovely her temporary home would be. The woman told her, "I'm going to give you two words to remember. Before I leave, I will ask you to tell me the words." She, Aunt Jennie and her son went over several pages of paperwork before the woman said, "Well, I guess that's all for now. I will be in touch."

Aunt Jennie said to her, "I think you forgot something." The woman, looking embarrassed, said, "I did?"

"Yes, but I remembered the two words," said my aunt, quite pleased with herself, "jelly and pencils."

When I spoke to her on the phone, my proud Aunt Jennie told me, "Gordon said I did 'better than good' with that woman. I won't be living there, though. Even though my brain is okay, I need 24-hour a day help with everything else, so I'll be staying in my house until my new place is ready. Fran will continue to live with me until I move."

About a week away from moving in to Gordon's, Aunt Jennie wound up needing surgery on her leg. Luckily the operation was performed at a hospital near Gordon's home.

Currently, Aunt Jennie is in a rehab facility working hard to literally get back on her feet so she can move in with her son and his family.

Patience is not a virtue that my family possesses and this, I feel, is a very good thing. This character flaw will make my aunt work very hard to get back to her life so she can live out her days the best way she knows how. Dad's "baby sister" is truly an inspiration to those of us who share in the family bloodline.

Despite enduring many changes in the past nine months, the loss of her daughter, her husband, and the sale of the home Aunt Jennie has lived in for the last sixty years, she continues to amaze me with her strong spirit.

When I picture my aunt shaking her fist to drive home a point during an animated discussion, I see she still has fight left in her.

Go, Aunt Jennie!

Jennifer

When my eighty-four year old aunt was discharged from the rehab facility after undergoing hip replacement surgery, the physical therapist told me, 'We learned so much from your aunt.'"

With a wink, Aunt Jennifer remarked, "I thought they were more *with it* than that!"

Norman

*O*ne of the more interesting aspects of moving to rural New Hampshire was the discovery of the town dump.

There were no garbage men collecting the trash once a week like we were accustomed to back in Connecticut.

Here in our new town, many of the neighbors could be seen in their vehicles lined up along Route 111 on Saturday mornings waiting patiently to unload their barrels.

Most interesting and amusing to me was the fact that the dump was a favorite site for candidates running for public office to meet and greet the townspeople. This was the best place to receive handouts outlining their ideas to help them get voted in to local town positions.

After a while, we went to the dump only occasionally because we found out about Norman. He was the only trash collector in town. His truck in no way resembled the garbage trucks I was familiar with. Norman's pickup had rickety wooden sides and barely-working brakes from what I observed when he pulled up to our garage door. I was reminded of the character from Sanford and Son when I saw him.

We taped the envelope containing payment for his services to the lid of one of the barrels.

He'd jump out of his truck, wearing his beat-up straw hat and baggy overalls, held up by wide suspenders. After opening the garage door, he'd lift each barrel and dump its contents directly into the back of the truck, sometimes throwing a tarp over the whole mess before he pulled out of the driveway.

Norman worked quickly for an old guy. At his pace, he probably made quite a good living, charging two dollars a barrel, and no extra charge for the wave and smile he flashed on his way to the next neighbor's house.

Here was a man who truly seemed to be enjoying his retirement.

Joe

My neighbor Joe lost his wife to cancer five years ago. Although her remaining time was spent enduring chemo treatments, surgeries and physical therapy, I could hear the couple during the in-between times, through the thin walls of my condo, enjoying conversations together.

As his wife's illness progressed, Joe would tell me how Margie slept all day because her medications drained her energy.

Margie shared how she would watch TV all night because she slept all day and couldn't sleep at nighttime.

Still, there were two heartbeats in the house. Hearing Joe complain about the high property tax bill, and Margie's quiet voice calming her husband down warmed my heart. I sometimes closed my eyes, listening to them from my living room, as their words made memories of these ordinary moments.

Margie's disease reversed their rolls. Joe learned to cook and clean. He also did the shopping and laundry.

Near the end, when Margie got too weak to walk, Joe carried her down the three flights of stairs from the condo and through the parking lot to their car. He drove her to visit their daughter or to Boston where her doctors were.

Finally, Margie said, "Enough." There were no more surgeries; no more hospital stays.

After her death, Joe spent a trial visit at their daughter's for several weeks. The fast-paced lives of grown children and grandchildren were too much for him to handle.

Back home now, he fills his days with a predictable daily routine, content with his discontentment.

The Natina Pride

My **Father at 95:**

"Get that walker out of here. I don't want to look like an old man." (Posing for a photo on Easter 2007.)

My Aunt Blanche at 91:

I phoned Aunt Blanche whom I had not spoken to for quite a while. Her first question to me was, "How much do you weigh now?"

Momentarily speechless, I muttered, "Uh, I'm not skinny like I used to be."

She gushed, "I weigh one-hundred-twenty pounds and took up yoga last year when I turned 90." Barely taking a breath, she continued, "I do modeling, too, when the Veterans put on fashion shows."

My Aunt Mary at 90:

"I keep a hair pick on my night table so I can fluff up my hair when I wake up. I hate when I reach up and feel the hole where my hair is flat in the middle of my head."

My Aunt Jennie at 89:

"I have these horrible brown marks on my arms. The woman who takes care of me says not to waste my money on creams because they don't work."

Knowing she is on blood thinners, I ask Aunt Jennie, "Are they bruises from your medications?"

"Nah, the nurse calls them 'old-age spots'. I don't really care."

Then, almost as an afterthought, my aunt says more quietly, "They're *ugly.*"

You can't stifle the Natina pride.

The Folks

*O*ur family of five moved into our home in Windham, New Hampshire from Enfield, Connecticut the night before Thanksgiving in 1975.

It was late when we arrived, tired and a bit apprehensive about our big move. As we pulled into the circular driveway, we were welcomed by the light shining from the front porch the former owner left on for us.

We quickly went inside, got into our pajamas, and, with Dura flame logs burning in the fireplace, settled into our sleeping bags in our new living room as snow began falling outside.

The next morning we enjoyed our bacon and eggs on our camping plates since nothing had been unpacked in the kitchen.

Soon after we finished our breakfast, our doorbell rang. Two elderly women, each holding a pie, greeted us. They introduced themselves as Marion and Myrtle, "the folks from across the street." Marion told us, "We felt sorry for you and the kiddos not having anything for dinner today. We see everything is still in boxes."

We assured them we would be having a nice dinner and gratefully accepted their still-warm, home-made apple and pumpkin pies.

"How very thoughtful of you. Please come in."

Marion lived directly across the street from our new home with her sister Dottie and Mama, a widow. Neither daughter had ever married.

Myrtle and her husband Herman lived next door to Marion.

"We don't want to keep you", Myrtle told us, "so we'll be going along now."

"Come on over on Saturday to meet Mama and Dottie," Marion invited enthusiastically.

After the women left that morning, we placed the home-made pies on our huge kitchen counter and unpacked and washed the dishes and silverware.

We heard about a restaurant called the "Green Ridge Turkey Farm", where we could order a full Thanksgiving dinner to go. This was our plan, as we wanted to celebrate the holiday in our new home. The dinner was pretty good, although not up to home-made standards; but the pies . . .the pies made the day!

Two days later, we walked across the street and rang the doorbell of the little white house to meet the rest of the folks.

Marion greeted us with a cheery laugh, and told us to "be careful coming through 'the little house that Jack built.' All the floors in the place are uneven and none of the doorways are square. Most of the walls are bowed, but it's home!" We walked carefully as Marion led us through the indoor porch and into the kitchen that led to the living room.

Two smiling ladies welcomed us from their upholstered chairs in the tiny living room.

Marion proudly introduced us to "Mama". She was 4' 10" and weighed about 100 pounds. "Little Effie" was the affectionate name her friends used when referring to this ninety-something-year-old peanut. Effie's handshake was vice-like and her deep voice surprised me the first time I heard it. I found out later as we got to know one another, Effie Gordon met her husband when she joined the church choir. He was 6' 2" and sang tenor, while she sang alto. I never met him, since he passed away before I and my family moved in across the street. What a treat it would have been to have seen them standing side by side!

Dottie, the youngest sister sat with her hands folded on her lap, ankles crossed, and listened intently to the conversation. Her smile was serene and, to me, she bore a strong resemblance to George Washington. The hair style was similar. Dottie told us she had polio as a young girl, but managed to climb the stairs to the State House in Boston where she worked as a secretary.

"Papa dropped me off every day in the car", she boasted proudly.

Because the pronounced limp and weakness in her legs made walking difficult in her later years, Dottie never left the house. She busied herself tatting and crocheting doilies and afghans. I was always amazed watching her small, delicate, doll-like fingers creating such beautiful works of art.

Marion, a nurse for fifty years, worked on the hospital ship *Hope* before retiring. Her cheeks beckoned you to place the palms of your hands on them and chant "chubby bunny". She was always laughing and admitted, "Mama does the housework and Dottie does the cooking."

"I pour the coffee and wash the dishes. Since I was the career girl, I never learned how to do those other things." She smiled broadly, pleased with herself.

Effie gave birth to Marion at age sixteen, so they seemed more like sisters than mother and daughter.

Marion went outside only to get the mail from the box at the end of her graveled driveway. She told me, "If you're ever looking out your dining-room window and see me lying on the ground, please come over and help me up because once I'm down, I can't get up." This instruction was followed by a shake of her head and a hearty laugh.

I recall coming to her aid twice; both times she laughed sheepishly, brushed herself off, and insisted she was "just fine."

"How long have you folks lived here," I asked.

"Back in the 1930's this house was the family camp where we summered near Cobbett's Pond," Dottie told us.

The little house on Lowell Road became their full-time residence when they moved from Massachusetts in 1950.

Effie continued, "The indoor, side porch was a small store for a number of years where we sold dolls dressed in crocheted outfits and other crocheted and knitted goods. There were birdhouses as well as small wooden toys, all handmade by my son-in-law who lives next door with my daughter, Myrtle."

"Herman built their house all by himself in 1939. He added a long workshop along the back of the house that goes almost into the woods. They raised chinchillas for a few years. Myrtle set her alarm and got up every two hours to feed them with an eye dropper. They never *did* make money on that project, though."

I wished I had known Herman Baker before he got sick. He was well known in New Hampshire for his carved replicas of covered bridges and for predicting the weather.

Myrtle was the *take charge* sister. Marion referred to her as "our social butterfly" because she filled them in on the happenings of the town's seniors and Ladies Benevolent Society of the Presbyterian Church. Myrtle did their shopping and was very involved in the community, while the three ladies next door were house bound.

Herman passed away a few months after we moved into the neighborhood and we took the three ladies under our wings.

In the summertime, my husband Bob drove our lawn tractor over to the Gordon's driveway. The cart he pulled was piled high with vegetables from our garden and the ladies were delighted to choose from the bounty. Sometimes, he visited with them in their parlor, where Marion enjoyed the smoke from Bob's cigar that reminded her of "Papa".

The ladies had a routine. On Wednesdays, Ellie came over with eggs from her goose. They often shared them with us. One goose egg equaled two eggs from a chicken. The folks taught my kids and me how to blow out the eggs to make chicks out of them. Our home-made chicks decorated our dining room window sills.

Every morning at ten o' clock, the women served coffee in small juice glasses; half milk and half coffee.

One afternoon, when I stopped by, no one answered the door bell. I walked in, hesitantly, and all was quiet inside. I peered into the small bedroom, where the three ladies were still napping.

This room reminded me of Goldilocks and the three bears; three twin beds all lined up and each lady covered up to her chin in crocheted blankets. Dottie and Effie stirred when they heard me in the doorway. Marion was the last to awaken from under the blanket which covered her entire self. Her sweet disposition, always intact, Marion smiled and exclaimed, "Oh my goodness, it looks like we upset the routine!"

This was the most welcoming house I had ever walked into. The card table in their small living room always held a jigsaw puzzle for guests to entertain themselves as they visited.

My children loved playing at "The Folks' house." I remember one very snowy and blustery morning, I answered the phone to a cheery voice. "Good morning! This is Marion. I'll bet the kiddos are home from school today and they are probably bored. Send them over to play."

"Do you want to visit the Gordon's", I asked the kids.

Bobby, ten years old, Mike, nine, and Cheryl, five, couldn't get across the street fast enough. Each was intrigued with the dining room dresser with all the little drawers in it. "The two drawers on the right are special just for children", the ladies told them. Inside, were small carved toys, tops, horses and games from long ago. How they loved playing with these treasures. I remember calling the folks at five o'clock that day to have the children come home for supper. I could hear Bobby whining, "Do we *have* to?"

As the years went by, Bobby fixed their radios and installed new phone jacks for them. Mike mowed their lawn and helped weed Myrtle's garden. Cheryl helped both brothers shovel Myrtle's steps after snow storms. There was much give and take over those years, bringing pleasure to us as well as to them.

One year, we convinced the ladies to join us for Christmas dinner. Bob drove across the street and helped them into the car. He pulled in as close to our side-porch steps as he could and helped each of the women up the two steps to the porch and the final one into our dining room. What a delightful time we had with our folks!

Every year after that, we took our Thanksgiving menu to their house where they chose what they would have for dinner. My children delivered the plates of food to them along with the pie menu. The pies were delivered when we picked up the dirty dinner dishes. This became our New Hampshire tradition.

Myrtle was the sole caregiver of her family members, but never complained. She worked tirelessly for the community, too. She outlived her mother and her sisters for many years. She and I became very close friends despite our age difference.

I admired this woman so much. She readily gave up driving when she realized she was no longer safe on the road and gave up her much-loved home when she could no longer care for herself. Even after moving into a nursing home, she worked tirelessly crocheting beautiful and unique items for the facility's craft fairs. Her door was always covered with cards and notes from so many people who loved her over her long life and she still mailed notes and letters to people well into her late nineties. Myrtle was an avid reader, especially when her hearing became impaired. She was a very good friend to me.

That long-ago Thanksgiving morning marked the beginning of nearly twenty years of friendship and unforgettable times shared with our special neighbors.

The folks are gone now, but they are always at the top of my gratitude list. These wonderful memories come flooding back at unexpected moments, especially on Thanksgiving Day.

For Old Times' Sake

I haven't spent an entire weekend at the Jersey Shore since the summer of 1959 after completing tenth grade.

Now I am at The Ocean House in Spring Lake, New Jersey. I discovered it on the internet, thanks to a friend from Facebook. This Bed and Breakfast is gorgeous! It's a three-story Victorian, each room tastefully dressed in soft pastel wallpaper and bedding. I have been saving up for this long weekend for nearly a year, since I received word this fabulous place is owned by a former classmate and his wife.

Antique paintings, gleaming crystal and uniquely patterned china add elegant charm to this New Jersey resort, but the piece d' resistance is the enormous porch that wraps around the structure on two sides. Adirondack chairs, rocking chairs, deep-cushioned wicker chairs and sofas line the railings all around. I *love* porches!

Salt-air fills me with memories of going down the shore as a young girl. The ocean is only a block away. The Ocean House is especially crowded on this particular weekend. Since I arrived a day earlier, I am unpacked and totally relaxed on the porch, listening to the awnings flapping in the breeze.

As more and more guests arrive and climb the porch steps, I begin to feel nervous. Many of them seem to be on leave from a local nursing home and I'm not so sure they will be good company. I had envisioned mingling with more youthful men and women for the next couple of days.

I sit away from the steps on purpose, so I can glance through my sunglasses without being noticed. Most of the men have white, silver or grey hair while many of the women have not taken that natural route. My own hair is light brown, with hardly a grey in sight.

A few couples glance my way, as they head inside with their suitcases. I wonder if they are thinking the same thing about the woman sitting in the wicker chair watching them. Do we all perceive ourselves as youthful on the outside as we feel on the inside?

After all, this *is* our fiftieth high-school reunion.

Grandma Louise

$\mathcal{E}$very Wednesday, my cousin Louise babysits her two grandchildren. Louise is a no-nonsense, retired school teacher who is used to explaining things honestly and directly.

She arrives twenty minutes early one particular Wednesday at her daughter's house, letting herself in with her key. Andraya has left the soup pot out on the counter at her mother's request. Louise pours the home-made soup she has brought into the pot to simmer. By the time her picnic jug is washed, the school bus stops in front of the house and Bennett and Avery run up the driveway to greet their grandma.

Both children will have to change out of their school uniforms quickly since soccer practice starts in forty-five minutes. Grandma is busy setting the table for this early supper when Bennett asks, "Grandma, where is Eleanor Roosevelt?"

Scouring the cupboard for crackers, Grandma answers as only Grandma Louise, the teacher, would. "She's dead."

Avery, age nine, gasps, wide eyed and Bennett, looking baffled and momentarily silenced, shakes his head and very quietly and slowly tells his grandma, "No. That's where I'm supposed to go for soccer practice."

Louise roars with laughter, telling Bennett she has directions to the school. A relieved Bennett grins. Avery remains quiet throughout the meal.

As Avery climbs into the back seat of the car, she leans forward and admonishes her grandma. "You shouldn't have said Eleanor Roosevelt is dead. You should have said she was in Heaven."

A Gang Member's Story

$\mathcal{A}$ friend from my 1961 high-school graduating class calls me about once a month. During one of our chats, I discover this clean-cut, Justin Bieber lookalike had a tough side back then.

Johnny tells me a story about an encounter he and his gang had with some kids from a rival school.

"You were in a gang?" I ask incredulously.

"Oh, yeah. Ernie D. was our leader."

I am shocked at this revelation, as Ernie was a couple of years older than we were, also clean cut and smart, getting ready to go to college to pursue a medical career.

"We were 'The Gents' and our girlfriends were 'The Ladies'", Johnny laughs as he begins his tale.

"We wore grey dress slacks and blue blazers with the emblem, 'Gents', our mothers had embroidered and sewn onto the lapel."

"Anyhow, one night the six of us guys decide to check out the dance at Cliffside High. Shortly after we get there, a group of rivals waste no time escorting us outside, asking what we are doing on their turf."

Johnny continues, "I manage to slip away to call Ernie in Ridgefield for backup since we are outnumbered by the Cliffside gang."

"About fifteen minutes after my call, Ernie pulls up in his black and white 1957 Ford convertible. Parking on the corner, he gets out and, straightening his jacket and tie, walks up to the leader of the Cliffside group."

"He coolly says, 'Gentlemen, is there a problem?'"

Johnny laughs at the memory.

"'No. No problem,'" says the leader as he rounds up his boys and leads them back inside to the gym."

That's the way gangs operated back in the fifties. They talked the talk. Period.

Two Old Guys

Two old guys regularly frequent The Coffee Factory, where I like to spend time writing. They are there today, as I wait for my usual medium decaf. I settle in two tables over and try to tune out the loud, booming voice of the one I call *The Accountant.* He must have had some sort of accounting background before he retired because all I ever hear him talk about are finances.
He tells his buddy, "Say you have a $7000 investment . . . ." blah, blah, blah. Then he goes on with words like *extrapolating* which he enjoys using several times. I wonder if the other fellow is bored with this know-it-all and if he ever wants to get a word in himself.

As I begin to jot down some thoughts of my own, the subject changes at the men's table. I know this because the deep voice suddenly turns falsetto.

I hear him say something about "types of *old* widows." He mocks in this new voice, "See, my grandson Andrew mowed the lawn. Doesn't he do a wonderful job?" Then he chuckles.
The boring money talk resumes.

Before I continue my writing, I offer up a silent "woman's prayer" that he is a bachelor

Uncle Harold

*H*arold becomes my uncle when I marry his nephew. He is the George Burns look alike of our family with Walter Matthau mannerisms.

My little kids love him because he is "so cool" and doesn't act like an old man. Harold is an avid hunter who also enjoys cooking the game he proudly brings home in his hunter's sack. I will never forget the first time he visits us. He drives to our house in Connecticut from Pennsylvania with some game in his cooler. Soon after his arrival, my kitchen counter is laden with vinegar, brown sugar and many spice bottles.

As he happily sautés three squirrels in my good stainless steel pot, all I can manage to focus on, when I peer into the bubbling liquid, are their little knee caps! Since I grew up in the city, I view all furry animals as pets, and it is all I can do to keep from crying for the poor little guys cooking on my stove.

Later, Uncle Harold proudly places his delectable kill on the table. I sit warily, eyes squinted towards these poor little rodents lying on the platter.

"Go ahead. Try some", my uncle bellows. "Tastes just like chicken!" He laughs heartily at his joke.

I have to say, I can tolerate chicken more easily; maybe because *they* don't have knees.

When Uncle Harold is ready to leave for home, I tell him I will cook *him* a nice dinner the next time he visits. He laughs, winks at me and gives me a bear hug.

Lottie

*M*y elderly neighbor Lottie, who uses a walker, enjoys going shopping with her husband Joe. Joe prefers to shop by himself so he can get in and out of the store quickly.

"One time," Lottie tells me, "I went to the Stop and Shop with Joe. When we got inside, he turned to me and, pointing to the bench by the check out, said, "Stay!"

"*Stay*, I said? What am I an F-ing *dog*? But I said the word", ninety-year-old Lottie states proudly.

"There was a man standing behind me and he started laughing."

"He followed us all around the store."

With a twinkle in her eye and a smile at the memory, she adds, "I think he was hoping I'd say it again."

Leo

*A*nnual Town Meeting is an event I look forward to every March. The gym at the middle school is where we get to see everyone we haven't seen since last year's gathering.

So many people show up to voice their opinions and cast their votes on various town issues.

Mrs. Murdoch is well informed and long-winded. She is an annual attendee who demands answers from the selectmen as to why certain things have not gotten taken care of in a timely manner. She will sit back down only when they answer to her satisfaction. When she is happy with their explanations, she sits with a tight smile of satisfaction.

Old Mr. Hartland always comes prepared with a very thick binder containing minutes of monthly meetings held at the town hall, as well as letters to the editor of the weekly town newspaper arguing matters of interest regarding town affairs. He looks like a professor standing there with that open binder as he chooses the subjects of importance to him while the moderator stands at attention keeping a cool head at the podium.

My favorite meeting is the one in which Leo, the head of the cemetery trustees, pleads his case for more funds to be given his department. He is a serious man with leathery, weather-worn skin who takes great pride in keeping the cemeteries looking immaculate.

Other residents argue it is more important to allocate monies for education and ball fields. The discussions go on for quite a while, several people wanting the money for their pet projects instead.

When the moderator asks if any other citizen wants to add more comments to the discussion, Leo raises his hand, stands up and says, "I have one more thing to say. Let me put it to you this way: if you don't vote to give me some money for dirt, pretty soon the dead will be right up here with the living."

Leo got the money.

Aunt Jennie and Frank Sinatra

The following is my favorite "Aunt Jennie story".

"I was in my early twenties and so excited that I would *finally* get to see Frank Sinatra! My best friend Josie and I had tickets to the Palace Theatre in New York City."

"We got all dolled up in our best dresses and high heels and spent hours styling our hair."

"We saved up a long time for that night, but it was worth it because we were in the first row balcony seats."

"I don't remember who performed the opening act, but he was a pretty good singer."

"*Finally*, 'Ol' Blue Eyes' came out on the stage. I was so excited, I thought I would fall right over the balcony rail!"

"He turned to the left and said 'Welcome, my paisons; good to see ya.'"

"Then, turning to his right, gave a big wave to 'my neighbors from Hoboken, NJ'."

"When he looked up towards the balcony, I thought I would faint, *until he said, '*Oh, there's a bunch of *Polacks;* that's why they're stuck all the way up there.'"

Here comes my favorite part of her story about that night.

"I stood up, and shook my fist, and yelled, 'You son of a bitch! I waited my whole life to see you, but, you know what? I'm leaving, because you *stink!*"

"Then I grabbed Josie's hand and we stormed out of the theatre."

"All these years later, I still say he was a jerk."

Nana Mary

Whenever Nana came to visit for a few days, we played Canasta.

She brought her automatic card shuffler to mix up all the cards in the two decks needed for her favorite game.

The game consisted of laying down rows of cards that equaled points. You started out by having to "meld", that is, open with so many points before you could begin matching rows.

One of Nana's rules was "you can never go out concealed hand." You had to place your cards on the table for all to see. This enabled other players to see which ones you needed, thereby making it more difficult for you to get your hands on them.

Every now and then, Nana went out "concealed hand." When we protested, she just smiled.

One night I had the opportunity to do the same. "Canasta", I shouted proudly, as I laid down my winning hand.

My sweet nana exclaimed, "Damn! Now see what you made me do?"

I was amused, but knew Nana was really upset. I never heard her swear before.

The next morning, I found out just how much grief my concealed hand had caused her.
She sleepily declared, "I stayed up half the night saying *two* rosaries instead of one because you made me swear."

I guess rules are meant to be broken only by an exclusive few; in this case, my eighty-seven-year-old grandmother.

Senior Ticket

Something funnier than the movie happens on a recent night out with the girls. Before I get into all that, let me introduce you to the women who gather for these monthly get-togethers.

Julie usually does the picking up of our dinner on her way over from her house. Julz, as she is affectionately called, is the youngest of our group at forty something and holding until her birthday arrives in May. She is sweet, funny and best of all, knows how to let life just roll gently over her shoulders. She is slow to rattle and very wise in her attitude in accepting people just the way they are.

Dianne, my friend and neighbor, lives two doors down from my condo unit. She is the oldest of tonight's group, but probably the youngest at heart. She is a dancing fool, and despite, or maybe because of knee replacement surgery, goes dancing most Saturday nights. Tonight, though, we are graced with her presence. She is tall with a bubbly personality.

Diane (spelled with one n), my friend of sixteen years and a former co-worker, lives out of town now, so she will be staying overnight at my house. She is older than Julie, but younger than me and proud of her size-four frame and her petite height of five feet even. Her skincare regimen keeps her smooth and belies her fifty five years. She is the cute one of the bunch, known to us as "Little Di". She is mostly serious, but when she laughs, she laughs the loudest.

Once a month or so, I plan a night with the girls. Everyone gathers at my house because I know how to have fun cheaply and am usually the organizer. Most of the time, we stay in and play Scrabble, or wind up just gabbing and laughing.

We sometimes enjoy watching old movies I've purchased for a dollar apiece at the monthly used book sale at the library. We watch while we eat. If we're feeling skinny, we order Chinese take out. We have salad if we're feeling fat. In either case, we enjoy a glass or two of wine with whatever we're having.

"Something's Gotta Give", a romantic comedy, is playing at the Flagship Cinema, so we pile into Little Di's SUV for the one-mile trip to the movie theater. Julie waits by the concession stand after purchasing her ticket. Di is next, and Dianne and I follow.

While Julie waits for her popcorn, Di asks, "How much was your ticket?" Julz answers, "Eight bucks." I say, "Being a senior citizen isn't so bad sometimes. My ticket was only $5.50." Di, visibly distressed, announces, "*Mine* was $5.50." Dianne and I look at one another and burst out laughing. I say, "Di, it's the hat", trying to make her feel better. We wore winter hats because it was snowing hard when we left my house.

Jack Nicholson and Diane Keaton are a riot in the movie about a swinger used to dating women under 30, who winds up falling for his latest conquest's mother.

When the movie ends and we get back to my parking lot, Julie decides to go home as she has to work the next day.

As soon as the three of us get into my condo building, Little Di is phoning her husband on her cell phone. "Guess what, Tom? I was charged for a senior citizen's ticket at the movies!" Clearly, the comedy has not helped her to get over this insult. Dianne and I try not to giggle as we walk ahead of her. We break up, though, when we hear Tom on the other end of the phone say, "Well, Diane, I wouldn't *brag* about that if I were you."

When we reach the top floor, Dianne says "goodnight" and Little Di and I walk down the hall to my place.

Di gets into her pajamas and goes to bed soon after we get inside.

I stay up and have a cup of tea, still laughing.

The next morning, Di suggests a matinee for next month, where all tickets are one price.

The Neighbors

My eighty-two year old neighbor is quite deaf, so I can easily hear the conversation he is having in the hallway with the woman who lives across from me.

Evelyn: "I haven't seen you for a while, Jim. What's new?"

Jim: "Aw, nothin'. I'm just waitin' to die at this point in my life."

Evelyn: "Maybe you should run for political office. That would keep your blood flowing."

Jim: "No. I think it's better to *die*."

Sandra

"*W*hen I was a young woman, eighty-nine year old Sandra relates, I babysat for my sister's kids."

"One night, I took the bus home from her house and got off about two o'clock in the morning."

"As I walked down the block, I saw a man standing in a doorway."

"He said, 'Hey, Baby. I got something for ya.'"

"I said, 'Oh yeah? Shove it up your ass!'"

Laughing, she continues, "He didn't know whether to zip up or stand there like that. I guess no one ever said that to him before."

"My son hates it when I tell that story, but I get a kick out of remembering the look on that guy's face", she says with a smile.

"Of course, I would never talk like that now. But when I was younger, well, that was a different story. I wasn't afraid of *anything*."

Audrey

*A*udrey Larson has left a message on my answering machine.

"Good morning. It's Audrey," her call begins. "I have all of my canning recipes on the kitchen counter and have finally found the one for the *end-of-garden* relish."

"You can pick it up, if you come over today. However, I will not be home until late this afternoon. Jane is bringing me to my doctor's appointment, and then we are going to check out the new Goodwill Store on Main Street."

She continues, "Oh, by the way, Doris brought me some of her home-made leek soup yesterday. I will enjoy it for my breakfast. No, wait! Not my breakfast, my supper. Yes, for my supper tonight."

"Well, dear, you have a good day. I'll leave the door unlocked in case you come for the recipe. So long." The long message has ended.

I have a bit of a problem with this phone call. I have *no idea* who Audrey Larson is. She has obviously misdialed.

Her name and number appear on my caller ID, so I dial to leave her the message she has reached the wrong person.

To my surprise, she answers her phone.

"Hello? Audrey?" I ask.

She cheerfully responds, "Yes, it is!"

When I tell her I believe she has made a mistake in dialing my number, she answers brightly, "You're probably right. I'm 97 years old and sometimes, you know, I *do* things. What is *your* name?"

When I tell her, she says, with a chuckle, "Well, Eunie, I am very glad to meet you. You must come to my house for a visit."

She proceeds to give me her full name and address as well as the color of her house and its proximity to a prominent monument in town.

I am dismayed to hear her giving these directions to a complete stranger and am glad that I'm the one hearing all of these details.

Knowing this woman is confused, I tell her I would love to meet her some time, but will call her first.

She says cheerfully, "Lovely, dear. So long," and hangs up the phone.

Audrey is on my mind for the rest of the day. I wonder how and if I should try to find one of her relatives. This old lady probably shouldn't be living alone. She is obviously confused and should not be telling strangers where she lives.

The more her happy voice plays in my mind, the more I decide to mind my own business. She is happy and friendly enough to probably have many people in her life who keep in touch with her on a daily basis.

I'm glad to have had this brief encounter with Audrey and will add her name to my "Warm Fuzzy" jar.

Simply Retired

*A*fter three surgeries, I lost the vision in my "good" eye and had to give up my part-time job. I could still do the work, but was unable to drive at night or in heavy rain or snow, and, without a set schedule, I was forced to retire.

As it turned out, my situation opened up a great opportunity for me. The Association for the Blind got me magnification computer software and I began, in earnest, to write the book I had been working on for years.

A neighbor in my condo building drove me to the library where I attended my first meeting of The Creative Women's Writers Group of Greater Derry. Lynne, one of the members, offered to drive me home; our friendship was forged from that first meeting. Someone is always willing to pick me up and bring me home again. Three of us meet once a month, in between our regular meetings, to help one another in the creative writing process.

After my eye healed from all of my surgeries, I was able to drive again. Although restricted in how far I could drive within my comfort zone, my independence was restored enabling me to become more involved in my community.

More friendships were forged when I joined an exercise group that meets twice a week.

I have hosted book signings in town to proudly share my first published book, a memoir about growing up in Jersey City, New Jersey.

Once a month, I share a few memories from my book with the residents of Pleasant Valley Nursing Home, where the folks there share their own memories with me.

My condo is in a perfect location. The city girl in me is satisfied with lots of shopping places nearby as well as easy access to my favorite place to write, The Coffee Factory. This popular gathering place is a wifi-equipped haven where local artists' works are displayed on the salmon-colored walls.

Driving in the opposite direction from shopping areas, there is another peaceful place for enjoying the outdoors. Beaver Lake, a community beach, has it all; sand, lawn, shade, picnic tables, a glider, swings for the kids, a snack bar, and kayaks and canoes for rent. An added bonus; all this is about a mile from my home.

If I choose to stay home, I am blessed with air conditioning and a deck overlooking a sloped lawn leading to a pond surrounded by flowering bushes. I can also walk up the hill to my pool or just find a peaceful place on my beautifully manicured property under one of many large trees, or on one of the many benches dotting the landscape.

My other pleasure is connecting with my family and friends on Facebook or listening to audio books while I'm doing my household chores.

My iPod is a favorite possession. I can "chill out" or work myself into a disco frenzy, dancing in my kitchen, gracefully moving along in my socks.

A Kindle Paperwhite, my latest favorite possession, gifted to me by my daughter, brings hours of pleasure, even if the power goes out!

My cat Molly fills my days with her funny antics. She rattles my kitchen cabinet door to remind me to fill her food bowl, howls to let me know she has finished using her litter box and wants me to clean it promptly. She is quite a conversationalist, too, staring up at me "talking" if I spend too much time listening to the TV. instead of paying attention to her. At day's end, she curls up at the foot of my bed and keeps me company all night long.

While I do not have the means to travel the world, my life is made up of small things that live large within me. I am content to be "*simply* retired."

Granny D

*D*oris Haddock was born in Laconia, New Hampshire in 1910. I first heard about her in 2000, when she was known as "Granny D."

She believed strongly in campaign finance reform, deciding, just shy of her ninetieth birthday, to promote her cause. This dynamic woman walked ten miles a day across the country covering thirty-two-hundred miles before ending her fourteen-month journey in Washington, DC.

When the Democratic nominee for the New Hampshire Senate decided not to run just days before the filing deadline, Granny D stepped up and ran against popular Republican candidate, Judd Gregg. I watched the debate and that little lady never missed a beat! She didn't win, but earned thirty-four percent of the votes.

Granny D. lived a very involved life for one-hundred years and left us with this inspiring quote: **"If you have the power of one, you can do anything."**

Aunt Eve

*A*unt Eve has been blessed with good genes and is our oldest family member.

"I rarely go to the doctors and have never been admitted to a hospital," Aunt Eve boasts proudly.

She is still fit enough to bowl in a weekly league. I'm talking *Jersey girl* bowling balls; not the small candlepin types.

A wonderful seamstress, Aunt Eve still sews beautiful bridal gowns and other garments for her many clients.

Gardening is another of her passions. She tends to her co-op garden, often taking on weeding and picking vegetables in her friend's garden when he's away on business.

Her cheerful voicemail lets me know she is probably out with friends. She has many friends because she is wonderful company. Aunt is always the star at family gatherings and is often one of the first people to hold a new baby.

When we spoke on the phone yesterday, she confided she has let her hair turn grey. I'm sure she will still look vibrant and beautiful when I see her in a couple of months at my nephew's wedding

It's easy to forget our special aunt is celebrating her ninety-fifth year.

Neckties

I'm pretty sure mine was the only Dad in the world who loved getting neckties for Christmas.

Road Trip

Gene is a gregarious guy with a ready smile. He is impeccably groomed whether he's dressed for a special occasion or hanging around in his shorts and golf shirt. He has been widowed twice and is now courting Vinci, a well dressed, outgoing widow who lives on the next block of the mobile-home community.

Vinci has one major flaw; she almost *never* stops talking. It doesn't matter if the women at the pool are sunbathing or pretending to be asleep. Vinci talks to them anyhow. A two-way conversation doesn't seem that important to her.

Lillian, who has known Vinci since the second grade, accepts that her 78 year old friend will never change her ways. Lillian's husband Joe is very hard of hearing, so Vinci's habit doesn't faze him at all.

The four of them embark on a five-day car trip from New Hampshire to Canada. When they return, Gene relays the following episode of one of their daily jaunts in the car.

"I'm driving and Joe is sitting next to me with his hearing aids turned off so he can enjoy a nap before he takes over some of the driving. Vinci is talking, as usual, and a few times, Lillian tries to get in a word or two. Usually I can tune her out, but she's right behind me until all I can hear is yak, yak, yak, yak. Finally, Lillian gets her chance to tell a story and Vinci starts talking at the same time. Now I'm listening to *both* of them with the yak, yak, yak."

"I pull over to the side of the road, turn around, and say, 'For heaven's sake, Vinci, you're both talking at once. How can either of you hear what the other is saying?'"

Vinci answers in her usual calm manner, "It doesn't matter, Gene; as long as we *get it out.*"

Gene concludes, "What the heck could I say to *that*? I just shook my head, threw my hands up, put them back on the steering wheel, and got back on the road."

"After I turned the radio up a little louder, the din in the back seat was no worse than the sound of the tires."

Then, thoughtfully, Gene concludes, "Yeah, we had a very nice time."

Phoning My Dad

*D*ad always said I could call him "any hour of the day or night."

When he got older and took a little longer to get to his telephone, he'd remind me to "let it ring ten times to give me a chance to answer."

One day, after doing just that and getting no answer, I hung up.

Later on, when I called again and reached him, I told him I had tried calling earlier.

"I know", he replied, "I was *right here*."

When I asked, "Why didn't you answer?"

"You hung up on nine," Mr. Smarty Pants informed me!

Eternal Optimist

*W*ell into his nineties, my father always bought green bananas.

The Excursion

The light on my answering machine is flashing when I get home from my writers' group meeting. I push the "play" button to listen to the message. As I take off my jacket and toss my keys onto the hallway table, I hear the familiar singsong voice of my Florida cousin, Tyrone, who lives a short distance from my Dad's nursing home, I hold my breath for a couple of seconds.

"Hi Eunie, it's **Ty**rone."

He always puts the emphasis on the first syllable of his name.

"I took your father to get his photo ID today. Okay. Bye."

"Whaat?" I'm thinking aloud. My ninety-five-year-old father spends much of his day in a wheel chair. Cousin Ty isn't in much better shape himself, although his demeanor belies his 56 years. He has a crippling disease that bends his spine. When he has to look sideways, he turns his entire body to the left or right because his neck is frozen in place. He took my father out in the car to get a photo ID?

Because his physical condition prevents him from living what most people consider a normal life, Ty doesn't have many friends. He spends hours with Dad and the other residents from the Assisted Living/Nursing Home. The huge building houses both facilities, but everyone knows Tyrone and Gene.

I put the kettle on for tea. As I take the phone off the cradle and hit the speed-dial, I choose a decaf tea bag.

Dad, "The Chief", is always in charge of his nephew. That's why the phone conversation tonight goes like this:

"**Hel** lo," a male voice answers.

"Hey Tyrone, it's Eunie," I say, trying to sound calm. "I just got home from a meeting. I hope I'm not calling too late."

"Well, I *am* kind of tired, but it's okay. Your father and I ran quite a few errands today."

"Where did you guys go?" I ask trying not to choke on my cup of decaf.

"Well, since we can't find Uncle Gene's driver's license, I took him to the motor vehicle place to get him a new photo ID. The nursing home needs a copy of it."

"How did you manage to get him in and out of your car?"
"It was a bit of a struggle. He had trouble standing and I couldn't hold him very well. After we tried a second time, a couple of guys came out of Motor Vehicle and said to Uncle Gene, 'Sir, we can come to your home in about a week and take your picture there.' However, Uncle Gene said he would try one more time. He managed on the third try and got into the wheelchair. The men held the door open for him and we only had to wait a few minutes. Uncle Gene gave them his social security number and they found him in the system right away. It took a couple of tries to get the picture right though, because the first time, he was looking to the side, and the second time, he wasn't smiling. It looks pretty good now.

Since motor vehicle was right across the street from 'Eye Care', Uncle Gene wanted to get his eyeglasses adjusted, so we went over there. It turns out his frames are too bent to adjust, so we ordered a new pair of glasses."

Oh, geez, I'm thinking. Since I take care of all Dad's bills and oversee his medical appointments. I cringe when they make decisions without consulting me first. My other issue is, both of these guys are prime targets for rip-off artists.

I take a deep breath before asking, "Are they going to send me the bill?"

"No, he put it on his Discover Card. I offered to pay for them, but Chief said he'd put it on the card."

I forgot that my Dad is running around with a couple of credit cards in his wallet. I prayed these two had not headed over to Macy's afterwards.

Hesitating, and taking in another deep breath, I summoned the courage to ask, "How much *are* the new glasses?"

"Four hundred thirty dollars. They're very stylish and open up his face, where the old ones hid his eyes."

The lump in my throat is too big to allow me to say anything.

Thanking God neither of them fell down or got hurt, I'm glad they had a good time and got home safely.

But Tyrone is not finished describing the day's events He continues, "Then we went to the hardware store." A little voice inside me asks, *"Are you kidding me?"*

"What for?" I ask a little louder than I intend.

"Wheel chair extenders."

I have *no* idea what he's talking about.

"Physical therapy charges $40 a pair for them. Your father says that's too much money and he will make his own. Since he used to be a pipe fitter, he says he can make them out of PVC pipe and it will cost $2.00 a pair that way."

After playing what seemed like "Twenty Questions", I found out what these extenders are. They fit onto the brake handles of the wheel chair so the person doesn't have to lean over to lock or unlock the chair. I'm really impressed and proud of my old man.

"How did my dad manage to get in and out of the car again?" I ask.

"Oh, he waited in the car while I went in. It was pretty hot outside, but he was okay when I got back."

An *"oy vey"* escapes my lips, despite the fact I am not Jewish. I know I will need another decaf before this call ends.

Ty continues.

"It was getting pretty late by then, so I asked Uncle Gene if he wanted to stop off for some soft-shelled crabs to eat. He said 'No, it's too close to my dinnertime.' So we kept going. We drove back to Savannah Court."

"Did you make it back in time for supper?" I asked.

"We did, but the nurse just about jumped down my throat when we came inside to the lobby."

"We were just about ready to call Gene's daughter in New Hampshire to tell her that her father was missing!" the charge nurse bellowed.

"I told her Uncle Gene was with me," he said angrily, "but she said, 'You're supposed to sign out.'"

Ty said, "I told her I signed in when I got here before."

I tried to explain that the facility was liable for my father's safety and they need to know what's going on with the people who live there. Tyrone was focused on the fact they spoke to him "disrespectfully" and so I gave up trying to explain anything.

"At this point", Tyrone tells me, "Carl, the janitor came over and asked me if I was all right. I told him that my heart was beating rather rapidly, but that I was okay, despite the fact my feelings were hurt."

I ask, "What was my Dad doing while all this was going on?" certain my poor father must have gotten upset.

"He was putting the extenders on his chair."

I cannot stifle a smile as I envision my Dad concentrating on the task at hand, oblivious to the bedlam surrounding him.

I thank my cousin for taking my father on such a great excursion and for getting him back safely.

"I hope you get a good rest tomorrow", I tell him.

"Well", he says, "I'll be busy again for part of the day. I have to go back to the hardware store."

I am afraid to ask, but I do. "What *for*?"

"Your Dad wants me to buy more pipe so we can make extenders for Fran and Lila's wheelchairs."

We say "goodnight" and I hang up the telephone.

Lying in bed that night, I'm almost giggling, picturing a gentleman and two ladies sitting side by side in a very elegant dining room with white PVC pipes sticking up from the brakes of their wheelchairs.

The Roommate

$\mathcal{I}$ think my father was afraid of his roommate at the nursing home, although he would never admit it.

Tom was a big guy who suffered from dementia and mostly sat silently in his wheelchair. When Dad said "Hello" to him, he never answered.

He had a habit of wheeling over to the foot of Dad's bed, parking himself there, blocking Dad from getting by in his own wheelchair.

When Dad glared at Tom and told him to "get out of the way," Tom stubbornly held his position. A few times, Dad tried pushing him out of the way, which only led to a commotion. Dad raised his voice; Tom became agitated and nurses and aides rushed into the room. At this point, Tom began swinging his arms trying to keep the staff at bay.

Dad was often taken out of the room, which did not please him at all. "What the hell's the matter with that guy anyway?" he wanted to know.

When things quieted down and Dad returned to the room, he often found Tom watching *his* TV; Tom didn't have a TV, and turned Dad's on or off whether Dad was watching it or not.

Since the nursing home was at full capacity, it was impossible to get the men switched to separate rooms.

One night, Tom became extremely belligerent and had to be taken to the hospital. When he returned the following day, he was so heavily medicated, he slept all day for several days.

Dad pointed to the bed next to his and told me, "There's a new guy in here now. He's very nice."

I didn't see the need to comment, so I just said, "Oh, that's good."

Tom passed away about a week later. When I came to visit Dad and saw the stripped, empty bed, Dad explained, "The nurse just told me that man moved back to Florida. He was a good guy. I'll miss him. Boy, that other one was a real pain in the ass."

Fleeting Thoughts and Random Senior Moments

Tough Decision

She keeps asking;
I keep saying, "No"

Will it be boring?
I don't think so,
not really.

A change of scenery would be
a good thing,
but I've been there before.

Why dredge up old memories
only to come back sadder
than when I left?

The getting to the destination
reminds me of long-ago days
playing chaperone on field trips.

What I really want is an adventure;
new horizons to experience
at my own pace.

I long to watch the sunrise
while drinking my coffee
on the shore of a still-sleeping beach.

I want to be a part
of the hustle and bustle of a crowd
in downtown Portsmouth or Burlington.

She keeps asking.
I keep refusing.

I don't want my day to end
before *I* am ready to say goodnight.

All these excuses are really
just excuses.

The truth is,
in my head, I am too young
for senior bus trips.

Him

Thoughts of him
drift in and out of my mind
when quiet moments
give me pause.

Memories of a wonderful man
who reached into the core
of the me who was lost,
and drew me out.

I told him once:
"You make me feel beautiful."
He answered, "Sweetie,
you *are* beautiful."
I believed him.

Because we were of a certain age,
I once asked, "How should I introduce you?
My 'boyfriend' seems inappropriate."

His answer: "Why do I have to be
your anything?
Just say, "This is Bob."
Perfect! I agreed with him.

All these years later, though,
There is still a part of me who wishes
He *were* my . . . . Something.

Reality Checks

Realizing I'm old enough to be that grey-haired kid's mom.

Singing "Happy Birthday" to my forty-year old baby.

Receiving a card from an old friend with the message, "Welcome to the seventies", and she's not referring to the era, but my birthday.

Enjoying the company of the elderly, and suddenly realizing they are my peers.

Googling "How old is Robert from Shark Tank", and discovering this cutie is young enough to be my son.

My Old Flames

My two old flames
are in Florida
living out the winter
of their lives.

Attitude Adjustment

I am appalled at how wrinkled my face is when I view it in the mirror in my daughter's sunny dining room.

My spirit is restored when I take off my glasses and take a second look.

Everyday Miracles

$\mathcal{I}$ am visiting my father at a mobile home retirement community in Florida. Colonial Estates is situated on a six-lane highway. There is no traffic light at the exit. Every day I head out in Dad's car for some shopping, I find myself holding my breath as neighbors wait ahead of me to make the left-hand turn that will lead them to Publix's grocery store. These old-timers scare me when they swing out onto the boulevard at a breathtaking ten miles an hour. Slowly, I exhale when all are safely riding, unscathed, down Military Trail towards the shopping malls.

The supermarket parking lot is usually a nightmare of cars going the wrong way up and down the rows in search of parking spaces. Safely stopped, I find myself holding my breath again as I watch frail, elderly drivers disembark from behind the wheel while trying to retrieve their canes or walkers from their cars without falling.

After a few relaxing hours of Mall shopping, I try to ignore the tightening knot in my stomach when it is time to go back to Dad's home. I hope to return without incident on the roadways before dark descends upon the early birds who are night blind.

Pulling into Dad's driveway, I park the car, and take the short walk to the community center to check his mailbox. When I reach the corner, I spot Irene's now familiar grey Buick coming down the road. She only drives around the park because she's deaf, nearly blind, and has trouble out on the road. Pedestrians are used to her as they step closer to the grass when she approaches.

After a ten-day stay, I return to my home in New England, where friends ask if Florida was relaxing. Their eyebrows raise in question when I shake my head *no,* and tell them I was too busy observing everyday miracles.

Who Was She?

She is so much more than my babysitter.

The old woman brings me shopping to New York on the train and holds my hand on the way to the A&P on the corner where she buys fresh vegetables for supper.

One day she is bathing me in the kitchen sink when her friend stops by to visit.

I am very young, but very embarrassed. Also, I do not like this gossipy lady friend. Her conversation is always mean spirited and everyone is beneath her.

Mostly, I am alone with the old woman who sews beautiful dresses for me. She measures my cousins when they come to visit so she can make pretty dresses for them, too.

She cooks and cleans every day and washes the dishes and pots. Sometimes, I get to dry. This makes me feel grown up.

Washing clothes in the deep, galvanized tub is a difficult chore for the old woman. I try to help her, delighting in rubbing the pants and shirts on the scrubbing board that stands in the tub of soapy water. Rinsing the clothes is something I don't mind doing, but wringing out each piece of clothing is hard work.

When it is time to hang the wash from the kitchen window to the clothesline outside, the woman takes over the chore.

I wonder, when I get older, if I will have to wear those black shoes with the laces like she and the sisters who teach at Saint Mary's do. Will I someday wear housecoats and aprons and never go anyplace to have fun? Does this woman mind living this life?

Sometimes when we go to wakes, she puts on her black dress, black stockings and black hat with the veil that covers her face to under her nose.

I wonder how you know you are an old lady and have to give up dancing, gowns and pretty shoes.

This old lady doesn't smile very often, and, when she sings, the song is a sad one. I think maybe she has never been young.

All these years later, when I think of her, I realize I don't know anything about who she really was. Did she ever have her own identity?

I only know she was my grandmother for all of my life.

Finding Love Again

We sit, legs outstretched
along the length of the sofa,
my back pressed against his chest.

I pretend to watch "The Rock" on TV,
aware not at all of Sean Connery,
but of my breathing
matching the rhythm behind me

My concentration is focused
on slowing my quickening heartbeat
and the rushing of jimmie-like pebbles
running up and down my insides.

I turn to face him, nervous,
wishing his little girl were here now
distracting us with a game she wants to play.

He smiles, calming my fears,
and takes me away from
a thirty-five-year monogamy.

Deception?

Retirement home. Was it trickery to use this name instead of "nursing home"?

My Father's Hands

Give me praise . . . Teach me friendship . . . Give me freedom

Show me strength . . . Give me love . . . Share the workload

Give me all he has

I have always loved my father's hands.

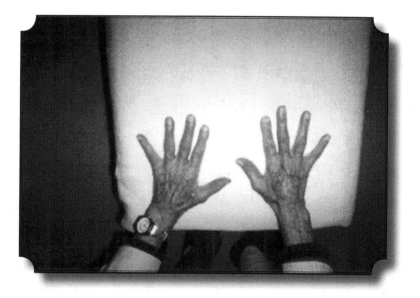

The Flame Still Burns

I took notice of him
when I started fifth grade
in 1954

He calls me from Florida
every six months or so,
which truly makes him my old flame
since it is now 2010.

The flame is much lower now,
but the embers still warm my heart
knowing he has not forgotten me.

Rude Awakening

I'm stopped at a red light
straining to look through my windshield
at the car in front of me.

There's something on the steering wheel;
a cotton ball

No, wait; not a cotton ball.
Someone's grandmother
driving that huge Town Car.

My eyes snap open
as I realize I've been dreaming
about Florida again.

Rest Home Lines

Lines of time on aged faces
hold memories of the times gone by.
Thoughts of bygone folks and places
captured tightly in mind's eye.

Knarled old fingers in laps lacing;
behind old eyes the memories tracing.
Etched in furrowed brow at times,
thoughts of past and valentines.

I see lines where some see wrinkles,
faces creased from winks and twinkles.
Even when the spark is gone,
I see lifelines holding on.

Sex and the Single Retired Girl

$\mathcal{I}$ heard a comedian joke about "when vaginal dryness meets erectile dysfunction." The audience laughs; I laugh, but am glad to know I'm not the only one who feels the relief.

The pressure is off! I feel the relief in not going in *that* direction again!

Surely I would feel differently if I were still long-time married, but I am a retired single woman. It's not so easy getting turned on by some elderly stranger. Growing old *with* someone familiar gives the illusion that both parties still look pretty much the same as they did all those years ago.

Don't misunderstand, I *like* being single. Maybe, one of these days, someone extraordinary will come along and change the way I feel about being intimate.

Right now, companionship seems more comfortable.

Coffee Shop Dreaming

Some day, I hope a nice guy walks in here, sees me writing and asks if he can join me.

The dream is to find "Mr. Wonderful", a fellow laptopper, a writer, a reader; perhaps even a *Democrat*! I am an author hoping to publish my second book in the not-too-distant future, having had my beginnings in this place of leisure.

I love being here at the coffee shop. I don't feel isolated, because sitting here sipping my decaf, affords me the opportunity to observe other people, and think and write without distractions that sometimes interrupt me at home.

There is no deadline or rush to leave this place.

This morning, there is a man working on his computer at the table in front of mine. He looks too old for me, so he is probably my age or younger. My newly-dyed reddish hair "youth-in-izes" me and I feel like sixty-something today instead of a decade beyond my hair color.

I would love to meet a man who shares my passion for writing, even if our meeting leads to a great friendship rather than a romantic relationship. My writers group of women is wonderful, but I would like to get a man's perspective. If chemistry happens to kick in, then all the better.

Mostly when I'm here, I stay focused on my book notes. Every now and then, though, I glance up, just in case *all* of my expectations are realized.

The last piece of lemon cake from the bakery shelf goes down so smoothly, it hardly seems possible it could have contained any calories. My coffee is nearly gone and high school kids are beginning to stream in, so I will take my leave. Since I'm retired, I can always come back tomorrow.

Vanity

The dentist advised me to leave my dentures out as much as possible for the next three days or so. I should have made an appointment sooner to have them adjusted, as my gums are now extremely sore.

My surgeon is the only person who has seen me toothless in all the years I have had false teeth. That's if you don't count my husband. I was married for about twenty-five years before I took my teeth out at bedtime, so technically my husband was the second person to see me this way.

I have placed a bright-pink post-it note on my door, which reads, "Teeth", so I will not accidentally leave the house without them.

Even in my late sixties, I would prefer being caught naked rather than toothless.

Vanity runs deep in my family.

Kay

She washed, dried, and reused the tin foil.

Maybe that's how she was able to buy all those dresses from the Alden's and Spiegel's catalogs.

Morning Joe

$\mathcal{N}$eeding to get out of the house for a mental health break, I head to my favorite writing place, The Coffee Factory.

I do my best writing there, occasionally looking up to see people coming in and out.

So much is weighing on my mind on this particular day, I am not terribly motivated to write.

I just need to be out in public where I have to hold in my tears and sadness; I call it "putting a face on it".

As I order my coffee and a blueberry muffin top, a man about my age starts a conversation with me about how he can no longer eat sweets or pasta because of diabetes.

As I set my food and writing materials on a table and sit down, he takes his place on a nearby sofa. He gets up again for a napkin from a dispenser next to where I am sitting and stops to tell me about a Seinfeld TV episode dealing with muffin tops.

When his story is finished, I tell him a friend mentioned to me that a muffin top has fewer calories than a bagel with cream cheese. He remarks "celery with cream cheese or peanut butter is good for you because it contains a lot of fiber and helps you go."

He sits back on the couch, looks in my direction and tells me, now that he can afford anything he wants, he can't eat anything he really likes. He shares with me he takes eight pills a day, has many ailments, including a couple of cysts in his head and suffers from vertigo.

Despite having undergone many tests by many doctors, he is not feeling any better. He is currently seeing an acupuncturist to see if his symptoms will be resolved.

When I ask if he has gone for chiropractic treatment, he tells me, "I'm considering trying that next."

Anxious to escape this rather pathetic exchange, I begin to write, and hope he will notice I am now too busy to continue our conversation.

As I write, he is still talking to me about fiber and how much better he is feeling at the moment after his morning "go".

I get up from my chair and hand him a piece of paper with the name and phone number of my chiropractor.

Taking the paper from me, he remarks, "Oh, you were writing *this* down. When I saw you were writing something, I thought maybe you were writing down "there's a weird guy in here, talking my head off."

I laugh, and then proceed to write this story.

Embrace With a Balloon

I visited my mother's grave. I attached a Happy Birthday balloon on the grave the day before. I said, "Mom, I need you. I worried you were in pain at your death. Mom, give me a kiss."

The balloon was on the ground because the wind was kind of strong, but it began to flutter up, up, until it fluttered in front of me. Then it fluttered towards me and touched my lips; the perfect kiss. I embraced the balloon. I love you, Mom.

Thank God for birthday balloons.

By Sue Rhodes 8/4/2011

Silent Woman at the Nursing Home

Beaded bags and Ascot ties
"Moonlight Cocktails"; gals and guys.
Polished toenails, Rumble seats,
Big Band music's lively beats.

Gowns and tuxes waltzing 'round;
dance shoes glide without a sound.
At their tables, others start
that old song, "Heart of My Heart".

She holds these thoughts deep within.
No one knows where she has been.
Quietly her memories roam;
woman at the nursing home.

Conversations About Life After Death

Gene: "I believe you will see those you loved who went before you and the ones who would have loved you if they had known you here."

Brenda: "I believe you will experience whatever you think will be waiting for you. If you are Buddhist and believe in reincarnation, then you will be reincarnated. I hope to see Da Vinci and Michelangelo and all those people from long ago."
Note: Brenda is an artist

Eunie: is afraid of the Catholic Jesus . . . "I hope it's true that I will see my son Bob and my Father and Mother and all my loved ones who have passed from this life."

I Wonder

What were his thoughts as he lay there
while the nurse tied the tourniquet
around his arm?

Did he wonder who would receive his blood?
Someone who had been in an accident, perhaps?

I wonder how the donor would feel
knowing his gift saved a 95 year old?

Would he mind?

I say a silent prayer of thanks for the person
whose blood flows through my father's veins.

Six months later, I say another prayer of thanks
for both of them as Dad celebrates
his ninety-sixth birthday.

Acceptance

$\mathcal{I}$ heard this brief, but heartwarming conversation on New Hampshire Public Radio. An elderly nursing-home resident was being interviewed.

The host inquired, "How do you cope with change at the facility where you live?"

The elderly man answered thoughtfully, "I ask what's to be done and what is my part *in* it and go from there."

On Turning Sixty Five

Being this old isn't so bad after all. I can now be and do as I please without worrying what anyone else thinks. I'm sure I've always been able to be and do, but now I am comfortable with this.

I shower, wash my hair and wear jewelry every day just to please myself. Today, I wore a gold and a silver bracelet on the same wrist and felt beautiful. I'm also no longer ashamed to wear rings on my bumpy, arthritic fingers.

I make myself happy in small ways, like eating by candle light, even when having oatmeal for breakfast. I love how my sage green dishes look on my eggplant purple placemats.

I'm grateful I can still see well enough to enjoy the landscape from my third-floor deck and watch the seagulls swoop past just before it snows. I capture the beauty of the New England seasons through the lens of my much-loved digital camera.

I'm confident and proud reading my own stories to my writers group.

People often comment that I am "cute" because of my outgoing personality. I *love* being "cute" at sixty five!

I'm learning to receive graciously.

Because I'm still a girly girl, I wear silk scarves with my sweatshirts.

I am most happy when I am disco dancing in my socks in the kitchen or waltzing with my imaginary love while Rod Stewart sings songs from the forties.

My women friends are as different as night and day and I adore them all!

I choose to do a jigsaw puzzle or two on my computer instead of cleaning the bathroom or doing the laundry.

I am more patient now; content to sit with Dad watching PBS at the nursing home without wanting to rush home to do other things.

My sixty-fifth birthday was much less painful when it afforded me a huge cut in my property taxes.

Being sixty-five is not the worst thing in the world.

The "Age of No Reason"

The "age of reason" *occurs when a child reaches the age of seven years. He or she becomes officially capable of knowing right from wrong.* This is what I learned in Catholic school while preparing to receive my first Holy Communion. This realization can weigh heavily on young shoulders.

A larger milestone was realized, when, at age sixty five, I reached the "age of no reason", another huge step in the process of living. *This* realization can *lift* weight from old shoulders.

I love this stage, when I can wear a goofy winter hat, for "no reason", just because I'm feeling playful, or giggle for "no reason" other than having just recalled something amusing.

"No reason" gives me the freedom to be the way I am without having to explain myself to anyone, and "no reason" to explain the tear falling down my cheek when I hear a sad song.

Most important, I have "no reason" to doubt the choices I make, whether they are right or wrong. The age of "no reason" opens up all kinds of possibilities.

Gratitude for my Birthday

It's the day after my birthday.
I view my Facebook profile
and am momentarily taken aback.
A voice within whispers,
OMG! I look so *old* now!

Then I realize why this is so;
I'm seventy! Wow! Seventy!
Slowly letting out my breath,
gratitude fills my heart
to have reached this milestone.

How I'd Like to be Remembered

"She made me laugh"

A Very Good Year

$\mathscr{F}$ranklin D. Roosevelt was the President of the United States the year I was born.

Soviet leader Joseph Stalin's photo appeared on the cover of Life Magazine on my birthday, March 29, 1943. The price of the magazine back then was ten cents.

Because of World War II, there was a copper shortage in the United States, so the penny was struck in steel that year

The Pentagon and the Thomas Jefferson Memorial in Washington, DC were completed in 1943, too.

Movies afforded people a welcome break from the trials of war, so honoring excellence in film and television was a fitting way to show appreciation by introducing The Golden Globe Awards. Many people flocked to the movies to see "The Titanic".

The average cost of a new house was $3600.00 and the annual wage for Americans was $2000.00. Forty dollars a month could rent you a house. You could buy a brand new car for $900.00 and fill it with gas for fifteen cents a gallon! Car registration was also introduced in this country in 1943.

An inventor from the United States created something that would have a major impact on me a few years later on Christmas morning: the Slinky! This wonderful spring toy and I spent many hours going up and down the two staircases in my house.

At war's end, I would be enjoying a popular stage in life known as "the terrible two's". Other little kids I would grow to love later in life would share that stage with me: Robert De Niro, Charlie Gibson, and Lech Walesa of Poland. Just imagine the fun I would have had sharing a big playpen with them, John Kerry, John Denver, George Harrison and Mick Jagger!

All in all, I would say, as Frank Sinatra did, "it was a very good year."

Final Thought

Life went by in a blink . . .

Acknowledgments

Thank you, seniors, who helped deepen my laugh lines. You make me glad I had the privilege of sharing part of your lives.

Thank you also to my family and friends, who continue to support my writing efforts, and to my fellow writers from the Creative Women's Writers Group of Greater Derry, who help critique my work and shower me with encouragement.

Special thanks to Carol A. Smith who photographed the author's portrait.

As always, I am grateful for my ever-present cheerleader, Cheryl Guyre who is with me every step of the way.